THE HOLY SEALING

Other Books by Anthony Sweat

FOR ADULTS

The Holy Covenants: Living Our Sacred Temple Promises

The Holy Invitation: Understanding Your Sacred Temple Endowment

Repicturing the Restoration: New Art to Expand Our Understanding

Seekers Wanted: The Skills You Need for the Faith You Want

Christ in Every Hour

FOR YOUTH

Q&A: Common Questions and Powerful Answers for LDS Youth (with John Hilton III)

I'm Not Perfect, Can I Still Go to Heaven? Finding Hope for the Celestial Kingdom through the Atonement of Christ

THE HOLY SEALING

UNITING THE ETERNAL FAMILY OF GOD

ANTHONY & CINDY SWEAT

DESERET BOOK

SALT LAKE CITY, UTAH

Image on page 55 courtesy Church History Library, The Church of Jesus Christ of Latter-day Saints. Image on page 71 courtesy L. Tom Perry Special Collections, Harold B. Lee Library, Brigham Young University.

© 2025 Anthony and Cindy Sweat

All rights reserved. No part of this book may be reproduced in any form or by any means without permission in writing from the publisher, Deseret Book Company, at permissions@deseretbook.com. This work is not an official publication of The Church of Jesus Christ of Latter-day Saints. The views expressed herein are the responsibility of the authors and do not necessarily represent the position of the Church or of Deseret Book Company.

DESERET BOOK is a registered trademark of Deseret Book Company.

Visit us at deseretbook.com

Library of Congress Cataloging-in-Publication Data

(CIP data on file)
ISBN 978-1-63993-486-7

Printed in the United States of America
PubLitho

10   9   8   7   6   5   4   3   2   1

To our parents,

DENNIS & BARBARA (HIATT) SWEAT
AND
JERARD & LILA (BAIR) BOHMAN,

who we are sealed through, respectively, into
the covenanat priesthood lineage as heirs,
and into the great network chain of the Saints.

And to our children and grandchildren,
through whom the same sealing blessings extend.
Our hearts turn and are bound to you, for eternity.

"I would advise all the Saints to go to with their might & gather together all their living relatives to this place that they may be sealed & saved."

—Joseph Smith, January 1844

CONTENTS

Authors' Note	ix
CHAPTER 1: THE DREAM God's Divine Organization	1
CHAPTER 2: THE GLORY Priesthood's Grand Secret	9
CHAPTER 3: THE HEARTS Uniting Eternal Love	22
CHAPTER 4: THE HEIRS A Covenant Lineage	42
CHAPTER 5: THE NETWORK Connecting God's Children	55

CONTENTS

CHAPTER 6: THE OFFERING
None Are Lost — 70

CHAPTER 7: THE MEDIATOR
Our Intended Condition — 84

APPENDIX
Promises to Posterity — 103

Notes — 109

AUTHORS' NOTE

It is October 7, 2022, and the two of us are on a hike in the scenic fall mountains of Hobble Creek Canyon, Utah. Although we are secluded on an afternoon getaway, through red leaves and evergreen trees, we see you. Not literally, of course, but as we walk and talk our conversation turns to saints and sealing. We have discussed this subject together for decades—really since we were sealed ourselves in the Logan Utah Temple in 1997—but the last few years have led to increased conversation between us on this pinnacle subject. Particularly after writing *The Holy Invitation* and *The Holy Covenants*, approaching the majesty of temple sealing was as natural as the mountain peaks now surrounding us.

AUTHORS' NOTE

But like those mountains, the elevated height of this subject is admittedly daunting. Sealing is so holy, and thus so sensitive; so mysterious, and therefore so misunderstood; so needed for everyone, yet so situational to anyone. That's likely why not very much has been published on it to the general Latter-day Saint. Sure, there have been numerous great books on creating a celestial marriage, and on spousal communication, love, intimacy, and the like. But not much has been written on the essential doctrines surrounding sealing itself, and what sealing seeks to accomplish.[1] Understanding sealing, however, is central to understanding the Restoration, the work of the last days, and exaltation. So how can we not at least try?

And that's where we see you. We see excited newlywed couples getting ready to be sealed and wanting to better grasp what it means for them. We see parents who are raising families in righteousness, but also some who are pained because their children have wandered from the faith. We see single members wondering where they fit in such a family-centric Church. We see gay Latter-day Saints confused or hurt about how sealing applies to them. We see members who have divorced and received a cancellation of their spousal sealing, sometimes remarrying and sealing to others, unsure of what that means for them or their children.

AUTHORS' NOTE

And, frankly, we see some who don't seem too stressed over sealing, feeling that love is all you need. Or yet others who feel really distressed by the concept of sealing and related songs like "Families Can Be Together Forever" because that celestial ideal doesn't match their mortal real. These, and many more equally important sealing situations, could each benefit from a book exploring the subject.

Our approach herein, however, is not to go directly into the many unique and varied familial circumstances surrounding sealing. To begin, there's a *General Handbook* section authoritatively addressing various situational "Sealing Policies"[2] that all can access. Secondly, there are simply too many unknowns. Great truths of the next world have been revealed by the Lord in His mercy, but it's often general, and not specific, and some vistas of eternity yet remain obscured.[3] If we aren't careful, we can quickly get lost on undeclared and speculative doctrinal wanderings. There's a responsible need for caution to stay on established sealing paths. Last, speaking of doctrine, we resonate with President Boyd K. Packer's timeless teaching that "true doctrine, understood, changes attitudes and behavior."[4] There's a power in eternal teachings on this subject that will allow the Spirit to

AUTHORS' NOTE

enlighten your specific questions and circumstances better than any other way we know.

We should say, however, that this book does venture deep into sealing's dense, beautiful forest. It has taken us many years to map some of these revealed but often less-traveled doctrinal routes, but their surroundings are stunning. On these pages we've tried to capture sealing's eternal scenery clearly—but also with helpful brevity—to give views of *what the holy sealing is doing, why it is essential, and how it blesses us*. To do so, we will explore in the chapters of this book God's work and glory, the priesthood, the marriage sealing of a man and a woman, covenant children as heirs, the great chain of the priesthood, the latter-day offering of temple work for the dead, and the centrality of the Lord Jesus Christ in perfecting God's divine organization. We recognize there is always more territory that can be explored, as sealing is so vast, and we look forward to further vistas ourselves. The Lord's prophets are the appointed guides in this sacred territory, of course. The President of the Church holds and governs the use of the keys of sealing[5] and "personally oversees its delegation to others."[6] Like placing cairns on the trail to keep us on course, we've done our best to base this work on prophetic words and the truths in the holy scriptures.

AUTHORS' NOTE

Speaking of words, you are likely noticing in this authors' note that it is "our" and "we." Although *The Holy Invitation* and *The Holy Covenants* were written by Anthony (with Cindy's invaluable input, of course), because this book deal with sealing, it was needful to coauthor. Not only is it impossible to separate our individual ideas from each other's after discussing these sealing concepts for so many years, but having both our voices provides expanded views and balanced perspectives from male and female, husband and wife, mother and father. It's better to hike this path together.

So, in that spirit, we invite you in these pages to come along with us on this expansive journey of sealing. The doctrinal colors are breathtaking. The eternal views truly are staggering. Sealing takes us up to the highest celestial peaks possible. There may be parts of this book that necessitate treading challenging theological terrain, breathing high scriptural air, or packing doctrinal gear that isn't easily implemented to fit your current circumstance. We're all at different places and paces on the covenant path. Regardless, we don't hesitate to say that in these pages there are evergreen insights for everyone. As you study the doctrines and principles of sealing, we believe you will draw closer to Jesus Christ and the power of His great redemptive work. You will sense Him walking with you no

AUTHORS' NOTE

matter your current family circumstance, as personal discipleship is not dependent upon your sealing situation.[7] You will see that *God sees you* and feel His justice, mercy, and love through His great plan.[8] Your heart will turn, as promised, to family—roots and branches—and the power of God's priesthood to connect, facilitate, and empower on earth and in heaven.[9] We pray that the truths expressed in this book can assist your sealing journey so that one day—through the blessings of the mountain of the Lord's house—we all are sealed up to glory in the eternal family of God, together.

>   ANTHONY AND CINDY SWEAT
>   October 2024
>   Springville, UT

CHAPTER 1

THE DREAM

God's Divine Organization

It is February 17, 1847, and President Brigham Young is dreaming.

Tossing about his revelatory mind with great anxiety was a question about "sealing principles."[1] Like Lehi, Brigham's dream took the form of a vision, and in it he saw the recently deceased Prophet Joseph Smith, sitting pleasantly on a chair. Brigham approached and grasped Joseph's right hand and said, "I do not like to be separated from you." Joseph rose from the chair and replied, "It is alright. We cannot be together yet. We shall be by and by."

In the dream-vision, Brigham noticed there was light to the south and darkness to the north, and that Brigham symbolically was in "twilight." The light seemed to turn his mind to the sealing puzzle at hand.

THE HOLY SEALING

Although Joseph Smith had implemented the broader doctrine of sealing in Nauvoo, it came line upon line and was yet underdeveloped[2] when he was suddenly martyred in 1844. In his life Joseph never sealed any children to parents. He didn't even get sealed to his own wife Emma until May of 1843, a year before he died.[3] Although essential sealing keys and ordinances were importantly passed on to others such as the Twelve Apostles, like the rising Nauvoo Temple, Joseph left a foundational yet incomplete sealing structure.

Brigham picked up where Joseph left off, seeking to forge the great "chain"[4] of linking the human family through priesthood sealing back to Adam and Eve (see Doctrine and Covenants 128:18). But the Church was not yet offering endowments or sealings for the dead[5] and thus was unable to seal people vertically through their biological family lines. They attempted to solve the problem by connecting Saints dynastically into the covenant priesthood lineage of God through the nucleus of latter-day prophets and apostles.[6] Was this the right way?[7] How do we create and bring everyone into the heavenly structure of the covenant family of God?[8] What can we do to help the Saints understand the binding together of God's children?[9] Such mysteries were on President Young's mind, and in his dream-vision he asked the Prophet Joseph his pressing sealing questions, saying, "If you should have a word of counsel for me, I should be glad to receive it."

Joseph stepped toward Brigham, looking earnestly at him, and kindly taught, "Tell the people to be humble and faithful, and to be sure to keep the Spirit of the Lord and it will lead them right. . . . If they will, they will find themselves just as they were organized by our Father in Heaven before they came into the world." And then, it happened. A monumental understanding opened, and God's divine order came into view for Brigham Young.

Brigham saw a great heavenly network. Not a network of rivers and roads, but of people and families—God's children "joined together" by the sealing priesthood in a "perfect chain from Father Adam to his latest posterity." In Brigham's dream-vision, he saw the celestial organization of heaven. Yes, heaven is *organized* and ordered. Would we expect anything less? On earth we mortals organize everything, or at least we try, lest chaos consume. We order cities and airports and garages and desks. We organize people into teams and reading groups and who brings snacks to the kids' soccer games. Masses don't coexist in harmony without structure, and cooperation only comes through organization. So why would heaven be any different? The Lord's house—His gate reflecting heaven—is a house of order (see Doctrine and Covenants 88:119; 132:8).

How, then, is the human family organized in heaven? Brigham said he saw "the pattern" of heavenly priesthood order, but then in an inexpressible summary simply said, "This I cannot describe, but I saw it."[10]

This I cannot describe!

Why could Brigham not describe heaven's pattern fully? Likely because—similar to other heavenly experiences—"no tongue can speak" (3 Nephi 17:17) such celestial things and "neither is man capable to make them known" (Doctrine and Covenants 76:116). Although Brigham Young couldn't find mortal words to describe the immortal order he saw, there's hope in Joseph's council that by having our "hearts open . . . ready to receive" we can be led by the Holy Spirit to deepen our understanding of sealing and its central role in exalting the children of God. Comprehending sealing is like understanding the Atonement of Jesus Christ. We know it is real and have experienced the Lord's divine grace through it, but like Enos we yet wonder, "Lord, how is it done?" (Enos 1:7). We may not be able to explain everything, but we can grasp the centrality of its reality and divinity.

THE DIVINE ORGANIZATION

So, what aspects of sealing can we begin to try and describe? Let's start here: Heaven's order centers on

THE DREAM

sealing—the securing of individuals to God and to one another for eternity by the power of the holy priesthood. Isaiah prophesies of "the increase of government . . . upon his kingdom to order it" that the Messiah will bring (2 Nephi 19:7; Isaiah 9:7). Sealing organizes the structure of the kingdom of heaven. The Church has taught that "heaven is organized by families"[11] and that marriage is central to the great plan of God.[12] Sealing perpetuates God's family-centric work and glory, binding hearts to heaven and to each other, to fulfill divine potential. God's work of salvation and exaltation is not only an individual enterprise but a collective endeavor, and sealing "is a welding link" that enables it (Doctrine and Covenants 128:15, 18). Sealing bestows blessings upon the covenant children of the Lord, creating potential heirs of exaltation. Sealing is the divine organization that facilitates the Lord's eternal reach and rescue of all of God's children so that none are lost (see Doctrine and Covenants 50:41–43). Sealing makes possible the dream to overcome the world,[13] endowing us with divine power through our oneness in Christ to conquer Satan. Sealing empowers the ultimate dream to inherit eternal life in the presence of God and the Lamb[14] and, together with our loved ones, to progress eternally. Like a divine mark, stamp, ratification, authentication, confirmation, validation, attestation,

THE HOLY SEALING

assurance, or signet,[15] in the order of heaven, sealing is everything.

CONFUSION AND DISORDER

Although the holy sealing enables these eternal hopes, Brigham Young reported in his sealing dream-vision that the prophet Joseph Smith lamented, "Our Father in Heaven organized the human family, but they are all disorganized and in great confusion."[16] Mortality is messy, especially when it comes to eternally connecting ourselves with others who have independent agency. Despite our best efforts, the fact is that nobody has perfectly clean family lines. All of us hit a Jenga-point where things collapse or fracture because of divorce, death, remarriage, singleness, or leaving the faith. As Bruce Hafen wrote, "It isn't easy to translate our doctrinal framework into daily reality, because mortal family life is by its nature a continual struggle between the ideal and the real."[17] The real includes a catalogue of Latter-day Saint marital situations that don't easily translate: single and never married, widowed, LGBTQ, divorced, married to a person of another faith, divorced but still sealed, sealed to more than one person, sealed to a spouse who is inactive, or unhappily sealed. Our sealing links to children create other issues, particularly when there is posterity who leave the faith or when there is divorce or death and then remarriage.[18] The doctrine of redeeming the dead opens yet even more challenges for some sealing situations.[19] The twilight of mortality creates so many sealing questions that the *General Handbook* requires an entire section with linked tables aimed at addressing the various needs.[20]

HOPE IN THE DREAM

Despite these challenging sealing realities, the dream of deep and everlasting family connection and love yet calls to us. We're wired for it.[21] Being alone may be nice for a quiet evening or a relaxing weekend, but heaven would fail in solitude.[22] The doom of damnation is separation. Loving relationships bring joy, both in time and eternity. The revelations of the Restoration help us see that heaven is sociality (see Doctrine and Covenants 130:2), elevating the nature of relationships.[23] Celestial living is both upward (connection to God) and outward (connection to family); loving God and loving others. And we're richly blessed that the restored gospel in its fulness uniquely provides both doctrinal teachings to support this relational yearning and authorized practices to cement it. We experience glimpses of potential eternal relationships while here in mortality—heavenly flashes of pure and deep familial love like a connective "array of power" from a union of

THE HOLY SEALING

faith and the Spirit of the Lord, as John Taylor said.[24] We taste eternity together, and it tastes good.[25]

Thus, let's never lose hope of the dream—that deeply embedded desire to "progress toward perfection and ultimately realize [our] divine destiny as [heirs] of eternal life,"[26] together with those that we love. Let's not become cynical or dismissive of the blessings of the holy sealing because there are challenges or ambiguities on the subject. Let's pursue the dream in faith, with hope, full of charity, and with a "sure reliance . . . to trust in the Lord and His love for His children," as President Dallin H. Oaks said, particularly on "unanswered questions about sealings in the next life."[27]

Although, like Brigham, we may be in twilight and can't fully see everything, we are certain of the light that has been given on some things: Jesus Christ is the way. Priesthood is the order. Family is the work. Sealing enables eternal connection. Pure love is everlasting. We are not alone. All are remembered in the covenant. Neither we, nor they, can be made perfect without one another. God's great divine plan is successful. Exaltation is possible. Family relationships can be perpetuated beyond the grave.[28] So, let's keep dreaming the great dream of uniting the eternal family of God in glory.

CHAPTER 2

THE GLORY

Priesthood's Grand Secret

It is September 7, 1842, and Joseph Smith is in hiding. Although an illegal[1] extradition attempt presses upon him, that's not what's primarily on his mind.

Tucked away in some corner of the home of his friend Edward Hunter,[2] Joseph was thinking about work for the dead, priesthood keys, and forging a generational link between the dispensations. Time on his mortal prophetic clock is ticking loudly, and the Seer desperately wants to help the Saints in Nauvoo understand what he calls the "grand secret" of God.

Do you know what it is? Apparently, neither did they.

"Now the great and grand secret of the whole matter," the Prophet wrote, "consists in obtaining the powers of the Holy Priesthood" (Doctrine and Covenants 128:11).

Joseph called this the "*summum bonum* of the whole subject," using a Latin phrase that means the "ultimate goal" or the "supreme good" from which everything is derived.[3] What ultimate goal stems from obtaining the powers of the holy priesthood? Joseph expressed this supreme end this way: "Herein is glory and honor, and immortality and eternal life" (Doctrine and Covenants 128:12) and "kingdoms, principalities, and powers!" (Doctrine and Covenants 128:23). *That is* ultimate, and therein is the secret we need to better grasp to understand the work and glory of sealing.

THE PRIESTHOOD ORDER

Too many of us do not deeply understand priesthood.[4] When we think of "priesthood," we shouldn't simplify or confine it to only male ecclesiastical offices in the Church, like being a deacon or elder or bishop. Those offices and presiding positions are important, of course, but they are what the Doctrine and Covenants terms "necessary appendages" of the priesthood (Doctrine and Covenants 84:29–30; see also Doctrine and Covenants 107:5). They aren't the *summum bonum* of priesthood itself. Let's not confuse an appendage with the greater thing. If you lost your finger (an appendage), would you still exist as a person? What about your arm or leg or ear? Those bodily appendages are needed and important, but they aren't your existence. Similarly, the essence of the holy priesthood is more than ecclesiastical Church offices. It is so grand that the Lord revealed the order of priesthood "is without beginning of days or end of years" (Doctrine and Covenants 84:17; see JST, Hebrews 7:3) and was "prepared from the foundation of the world" (Alma 13:3).

The *General Handbook* summarizes recent Church teachings[5] that priesthood is "the authority and power of God," that it can "flow to all members of the Church—male and female—as they keep [their] covenants," and that "God grants authority and power to His sons and daughters on earth to help carry out [His] work."[6] Priesthood ordinances—or sacred authorized rituals—unlock "the power of godliness" to be manifest in our lives (Doctrine and Covenants 84:20–21). Priesthood power, authority, covenants, and ordinances form the channel through which the fulness of God's blessings flow. Priesthood is essential to God's plan. The holy priesthood is summarized in scripture as "the Order of the Son of God" (Doctrine and Covenants 107:3). This order of priesthood includes both men and women.[7] An "order" is a group of people with certain qualities—someone who is part

THE HOLY SEALING

of a distinct classification.[8] In the case of priesthood, it is a *covenant order* of persons living a life patterned after Jesus Christ, dedicated to doing the will and work of God, who are authorized and empowered by Him. Thus, it is "the Holy Priesthood, after the Order of the Son of God," or what today we call *Melchizedek Priesthood*, because in that holy order "Melchizedek was such a great high priest" (Doctrine and Covenants 107:2–3).

Melchizedek was great for many reasons, but his righteousness was key. Literally, his name means "king of righteousness" (Hebrews 7:2) or "righteous king" (from the Hebrew *melek* = "king" and *sadeq* = "to be just").[9] He was a "king of peace" (Hebrews 7:2). Melchizedek initiated another righteous man, Abraham, into this covenant priesthood order (Doctrine and Covenants 84:14), by which Abraham obtained "the blessings of the fathers" because he too "was a follower of righteousness" (Abraham 1:2). And what did Abraham obtain as a result of becoming "a prince of peace" in this righteous priesthood order, like Melchizedek? He "became a rightful heir" (see chapter 4, "The Heirs") and received his "appointment unto the Priesthood according to the appointment of God unto the fathers concerning the seed" (Abraham 1:2, 4). As an heir of the priesthood, Abraham was promised that "all that my Father hath shall be given unto him" (Doctrine and Covenants 84:38) as a partaker of God's glory (see Abraham 3:26; Doctrine and Covenants 93:22). He entered into eternal marriage with Sarah (see Abraham 2:2) and with her was given a promised land (Abraham 2:6), promised a great family and endless posterity (Abraham 2:9), and given priesthood power, authority, and ministry that centered "in thy seed (that is, thy priesthood)" (Abraham 2:11). We call this the "Abrahamic Covenant," because it was renewed through Abraham, but it could just as easily be called the Melchizedek covenant, or Enoch covenant, or Adam covenant. It is the holy covenants and eternal promises of exaltation.

THE SEED

Notice in the preceding verses how the Lord connected righteousness to priesthood, and priesthood to *seed*. That is a crucial concept in our understanding of the *summum bonum* of obtaining the powers of the holy priesthood. Of all the titles God can use, "Father" is what He asks to be called.[10] Perhaps it is because His divine Fatherhood is central to His eternal glory. If we had to summarize Godhood in one word, it could be *parenthood*.[11] The work and glory of God centers in eternal family. Indeed, God's "work and glory" is "to bring to pass the immortality and eternal life" (Moses 1:39) of His and our Mother in Heaven's children.[12] While we often focus on God's work in that popular verse, we don't often seem to connect that God's *glory* centers in the power and authority (or priesthood) to bring up children to eternal life. Indeed, the Prophet Joseph Smith taught that through the work that God does with His children, God "obtains kingdom upon kingdom, and it will exalt his glory."[13] God's priesthood power and seed continue everlastingly, and thus His glory increases eternally also.

As God's offspring, we are promised that because of Jesus Christ and by living sacred temple covenants, we can be exalted and become like God.[14] We can be heirs of God, have His priesthood put upon us, and receive the exalting temple blessings of "the fathers,"[15] like Abraham and Sarah (see Abraham 1:18; Romans 4:16). And what does that exaltation and priesthood order look like? Logic follows it will be patterned after God's family-centric work and glory. Indeed, the Lord revealed that in eternity our "exaltation and glory . . . shall be a fulness and a continuation of the seeds forever and ever" or a "continuation of the lives" (Doctrine and Covenants 132:19, 22), just like God. Eternal glory is embedded in eternal seed. Eternal life is family life.

The lines below seek to simplify and connect these important but deep conceptual priesthood links—the grand secret and *summum bonum* of it all, which we seek to obtain:

- Priesthood is *God's power and authority*.
- We obtain God's power and authority by *covenant righteousness through Christ's order*.
- Covenant righteousness through Christ's order brings *eternal life*.
- Eternal life centers in continuing seed, or *God's eternal family*.
- God's eternal family is *God's work and glory*.
- God's work and glory can become *our work and glory through eternal marriage and family*.

ETERNAL MARRIAGE

As this doctrine of the priesthood distills upon our souls (see Doctrine and Covenants 121:45), we can see more clearly why priesthood is connected to eternal marriage or being "sealed" by the power of the holy priesthood to a spouse. When we enter the holy temple, we are washed, anointed, clothed, endowed, and blessed to one day become kings and priests or queens and priestesses if we live our holy covenants.[16] Through the covenants and ordinances of the holy temple endowment, we receive "power from on high" (Doctrine and Covenants 38:32)—or in other words, priesthood—to do God's work, overcome the world, and receive a fulness of His blessings.[17]

After being endowed, the culminating ordinance[18] of the temple is for us to "enter into this order of the priesthood [meaning the new and everlasting covenant of marriage]" (Doctrine and Covenants 131:2). No righteous man can be exalted without a righteous woman, nor vice versa.[19] There is no king without a queen, and no queen without a king. No solo monarchs reign in heaven. Godhood is parenthood, and exaltation is predicated on the uniting of the genders in an order of the priesthood eternally. Indeed, this ultimately *is* priesthood in its fulness.[20] This "new and everlasting covenant" of priesthood marriage was "instituted for the fulness of [God's] glory" (Doctrine and Covenants 132:6).

Sometimes this covenant priesthood order is called the "patriarchal order" or "pattern" of the priesthood.[21] *Patriarchal* is a scriptural term (see Abraham 1:26). Although scriptural, this term can become problematic today because the root of the word centers in governing by men, creating confusion or misunderstanding about equal partnership between women and men, particularly in the home.[22] Another way to describe or understand the patriarchal order is as an order of priesthood *family* government with a patriarch (man) and matriarch[23] (woman) working as coequals[24] in an eternal union to do God's work. President Ezra Taft Benson taught:

> The order of priesthood spoken of in the scriptures is sometimes referred to as the patriarchal order because it came down from father to son. But this order is otherwise described in modern revelation as an order of family government where a man and woman enter into a covenant with God—just as did Adam and Eve—to be sealed for eternity, to have posterity, and to do the will and work of God throughout their mortality.[25]

Without entering into this order of priesthood, we "cannot have an increase" (Doctrine and Covenants 131:4). Joseph Smith elaborated on this teaching when he said:

> Except a man and his wife enter into an everlasting covenant and be married for eternity . . . they will cease to increase when they die, that is, that they will not have any children after the resurrection; but those who are married by the power and authority of the Priesthood . . .

will continue to increase and have children in the celestial glory.[26]

Referencing this, President Dallin H. Oaks taught, "Eternal life includes the creative powers inherent in the combination of male and female—what modern revelation describes as the 'continuation of the seeds forever and ever.'"[27] This "continuing" of eternal posterity may be one way to understand how the priesthood "continueth" forever (see Doctrine and Covenants 84:18; Hebrews 7:24).

This blessing of a continuation of seed is central to what was promised to Abraham and Sarah, and (again) what defined the priesthood that Abraham so desperately sought. "In thee (that is, in thy Priesthood) and in thy seed (that is, thy Priesthood) . . . shall all the families of the earth be blessed, even with the blessings of the Gospel . . . even of life eternal" (Abraham 2:11). Through filling the earth "with the measure of man" the earth "answer[s] the end of its creation" (Doctrine and Covenants 49:16–17). Thy seed is thy priesthood, and thy priesthood is thy seed.

PRIESTHOOD RIGHTEOUSNESS

It is crucial to clarify here that this promise of priesthood isn't connected to just anyone who has children, nor is it connected to anyone who even enters a temple and gets sealed. While the priesthood can "be conferred upon us, it is true," if someone lives unrighteously, the Lord succinctly says "amen to the priesthood or the authority" of that person (Doctrine and Covenants 121:37). This is because:

> No power or influence can or ought to be maintained by virtue of the priesthood, only by persuasion, by long-suffering, by gentleness and meekness, and by love unfeigned; By kindness, and pure knowledge . . . without hypocrisy, and without guile . . . full of charity . . . [and] virtue." (Doctrine and Covenants 121:41–42, 45)

While there are many applications to the principles expressed in these priesthood verses, connecting priesthood to family is crucial. The patriarchal order can be conferred upon us through an eternal marriage sealing, it is true, but only those who learn to govern themselves and serve God and their families in righteousness will have power in the priesthood, in time or eternity. If priesthood centers in familial relationships, it is only by gentleness, meekness, love, kindness, chastity, temperance, and other righteous characteristics that families are sustained over time and throughout eternity. Those and other righteous principles

THE HOLY SEALING

enable relationships to endure. The revelations teach that heaven is not so much a place as it is an ability. Specifically, the endowed spiritual capacity to abide in celestial "laws" and "conditions" (Doctrine and Covenants 88:36–40; 132:5; Mosiah 4:8). If you live laws and principles of righteousness, through God's grace you can develop the ability to continue in eternal covenant relationships and "the doctrine of the priesthood shall distil upon thy soul as the dews from heaven . . . and thy dominion shall be an everlasting dominion, and without compulsory means it shall flow unto thee forever and ever" (Doctrine and Covenants 121:45–46).

Importantly, this promise of priesthood through the order of eternal marriage and parenthood applies to all the covenant faithful, including those who are currently single or childless in mortality despite righteous desires. We have been repeatedly promised by prophets that if we remain faithful to our covenants, all the blessings of exaltation will be ours, including the blessings of eternal marriage and family.[28] No opportunity will be denied the faithful by a wise and just God (see chapter 7, "The Mediator").

THE WORK

Are we starting yet to more clearly see the grand

secret of priesthood? Are we more clearly seeing its ultimate goal and supreme good?

As Joseph Smith taught:

> Here then is eternal life, to know the only wise and true God. You have got to learn how to be Gods yourselves; to be kings and priests [and queens and priestesses] to God, the same as all Gods have done; by going from a small degree to another, from grace to grace, from exaltation to exaltation, until you are able to sit in glory as doth those who sit enthroned in everlasting power.[29]

Yes, herein is the grand secret—in obtaining the powers of the holy priesthood.

Yes, herein is the *summum bonum* of it all—that priesthood is eternally tied to everlasting posterity.

Yes, herein is glory, immortality, and eternal lives—in uniting ourselves for eternity in a priesthood order of righteous marriage to obtain priesthood power to do the everlasting work of God.

That work will bring God's glory, but it requires covenant hearts.[30]

CHAPTER 3

THE HEARTS

Uniting Eternal Love

It is Monday, May 15, 1843, and a young newlywed named Melissa Johnson is expecting company at her home.

And not just from anyone, but from a visitor she knows as the prophet of the Lord.

Just a year and a half before, on Christmas Day 1841, twenty-year-old Melissa had married a good, faithful, twenty-three-year-old returned missionary named Benjamin Johnson. In 1843 their love was still so young and fresh it hung in the air like the May flowers popping up around their home in Ramus, Illinois, a small town about twenty miles east of Nauvoo.

Melissa had an ease of manner about her, and coupled with her culture, refinement, and love for the

THE HEARTS

Lord, it was easy to see why Benjamin was smitten.[1] Benjamin had a goodness about him, and together with his loyalty, hard work, and dedication to God, Melissa was naturally drawn to him.[2] Benjamin was also close with the Prophet Joseph Smith, and when Joseph came to Ramus, Benjamin said "he lodged in no house but mine."[3] And on this day in May 1843, that's exactly what Joseph did (along with his secretary William Clayton). His visit would prove to have eternal effects.

As the evening settled, Joseph called Melissa and Benjamin "to come and sit down." When Joseph was with the Johnsons there "was no lack of amusement," with the group often passing time playing games together, singing, and telling jokes.[4] But this particular evening, Joseph wasn't in a light mood. He was serious. Heavenly things were on his mind.

He told Melissa and Benjamin that he "wished to marry [them] according to the law of the Lord." Benjamin failed to read the moment and thought Joseph was kidding. Playing along, he said if they were to get married again, this time Melissa had to be the one who did all the courting (or dating) because, Benjamin claimed, "I did it all the first time." You can almost picture Benjamin rolling back in his chair and slapping his knee as the joke fell flat. Joseph "chided my levity" and "told me he was in earnest,"[5] recalled Benjamin. If Joseph didn't have Melissa and Benjamin's serious attention before, he surely had it now.

Although the Johnsons had been married legally a year and a half ago, they had not yet been sealed for eternity together. Not many in the Church had, or at that time had even heard of it, let alone understood the reasons why they should. So, there in their living room, the prophet Joseph Smith gave Melissa and Benjamin teachings that would be recorded and later canonized in scripture. He taught them:

> In the Celestial glory there are three heavens or degrees, and in order to obtain the highest, a man must enter into this order of the Priesthood, & if he does not, he can not obtain it. He may enter into the other, but that is the end of his Kingdom, he can not have an increase.[6]

Clarifying this "order" and "increase," the prophet explained:

> [If] a man & his Wife enter into an everlasting covenant & be married for eternity, while in this probation; by the power & authority of the Holy Priesthood; they will . . . continue to increase & have children in the Celestial glory.[7]

THE HEARTS

To a couple like Melissa and Benjamin, such news would have been sweet. At the time they had one son, but in earlier years Benjamin had worried he would never have children, saying, "Often I have felt to tell the Lord that if He would spare my life to see one son who would bear my name after me in honor to him, I would promise to die without regret; and it seemed that every ambition, hope or inspiration for life was swallowed up in that one desire."[8]

Building upon that familial desire and their love for one another, Joseph taught Melissa and Benjamin, "Our mission to the earth was to organize a nuclei of Heaven, to take with us, to the increase of which there would be no end."[9]

There, in the quiet sacred silence of their home on a spring day in May 1843—without wedding dresses and bridesmaids or songs and dancing and receptions—Melissa and Benjamin Johnson stood up, took each other's hand,[10] and were sealed by the Prophet Joseph Smith "in an everlasting covenant"[11] as husband and wife for all eternity.[12] A new family nucleus of heaven was formed. It was the most important day of their lives.

ANGELS AND GODS

As the Lord has revealed—and as Joseph explained to Benjamin and Melissa Johnson—being sealed in

THE HOLY SEALING

an eternal marriage is the most important day in our lives also,[13] as this ordinance is required to receive the blessings of the highest heaven (see Doctrine and Covenants 131:1–3). Without being sealed to a spouse, we are limited in our eternal progression, or we "cannot have an increase" (Doctrine and Covenants 131:4). Contrary to much modern societal messaging, we are not intended to be solitary individuals. God has designed us and His work on a plan of *interdependence,* not independence, combining the uniqueness of male and female to produce success[14] unattainable on our own in this life and the next. With our Heavenly Parents' pattern as the basis of our theology,[15] we seek to unite the genders. The family-centric work of God requires the hearts of a man and woman to be sealed together, as "neither is the man without the woman, neither the woman without the man, in the Lord" (1 Corinthians 11:11).

Yes, we are promised that the "same sociality which exists among us here will exist among us there, only it will be coupled with eternal glory" (Doctrine and Covenants 130:2). That sociality, however, centers in sealing. The Lord taught that "all covenants, contracts, bonds, obligations, oaths, vows, performances, connections, associations, or expectations, that are not made and entered into and sealed by the Holy Spirit of promise, of him who is anointed, both as well for time and for all eternity, . . . are of no efficacy, virtue, or force in and after the resurrection from the dead; for all contracts that are not made unto this end have an end when men are dead" (Doctrine and Covenants 132:7).

God's house "is a house of order, saith the Lord God, and not a house of confusion" (Doctrine and Covenants 132:8). "Every kingdom is given a law; and unto every law there are certain bounds also and conditions. All beings who abide not in those conditions are not justified" (Doctrine and Covenants 88:38–39). The law of exaltation in the celestial kingdom requires sealing a man and woman by the power of the holy priesthood. Otherwise, "their covenant and marriage are not of force when they are dead, and when they are out of the world" (Doctrine and Covenants 132:15). If we do not enter and abide by the laws of eternal marriage, then the Lord revealed that the highest glory we attain in eternity is to be "appointed angels in heaven, which angels are ministering servants, to minister for those who are worthy of a far more, and an exceeding, and an eternal weight of glory. For these angels did not abide my law; therefore, they cannot be enlarged, but remain separately and singly, without exaltation,

THE HOLY SEALING

in their saved condition, to all eternity" (Doctrine and Covenants 132:16–17).

Those who do enter and abide the laws of eternal marriage, however, are promised all the blessings of exaltation—a fulness of all God has and is. The Doctrine and Covenants expresses it this way:

> If a man marry a wife by my word, which is my law, and by the new and everlasting covenant, and it is sealed unto them by the Holy Spirit of promise, by him who is anointed . . . [they] shall come forth in the first resurrection . . . and shall inherit thrones, kingdoms, principalities, and powers, dominions, all heights and depths . . . and they shall pass by the angels, and the gods, which are set there, to their exaltation and glory in all things, as hath been sealed upon their heads, which glory shall be a fulness and a continuation of the seeds forever and ever. . . . Then shall they be gods, because they have all power, and the angels are subject unto them. (Doctrine and Covenants 132:19–20)

That's why President Russell M. Nelson pled for those who haven't yet been sealed in an eternal marriage "to take the necessary steps to receive that crowning, life-changing ordinance. Will it make a difference?

Only if you want to progress forever and be together forever. Wishing to be together forever will not make it so. No other ceremony or contract will make it so."[16]

NOT OF THIS WORLD

Thus, a holy sealing is much more than a wedding. It is also notably different from other legal marriage or ring ceremonies. Instead of wearing the latest wedding dress or suit, the woman and man are adorned in their sacred robes of the holy priesthood, representing their priestly status before God. The sealing doesn't take place in a rented wedding hall for parties, but in a gloriously dedicated temple for the eternities. The bride and groom don't stand, but instead symbolically and humbly kneel across from one another at an altar. There's no music, only quiet reverence. No valets handling car keys, but instead a sealer using authorized priesthood keys with power to bind on earth and in heaven. Vows aren't created and read by the couple, but instead God's revealed words for a sacred ordinance are spoken and agreed to in a solemn covenant. This ceremony isn't uniting only for time, but for eternity. Beyond bestowing wishes of earthly prosperity and love, the ceremony opens exalting blessings of Abraham, Isaac, and Jacob. Not just creating a couple under the law on earth, but creating a new nuclei in heaven. Yes, a temple sealing looks different than other marriages because it is—it is uniting covenant hearts for all eternity to do God's work and receive a fulness of exalted blessings.

THE HEARTS

Although romantic love is often the focus in modern marriage, eternal marriage centers on charity, or the love of God—a far more potent love that "endureth forever" (Moroni 7:47). A holy sealing is founded upon following the teachings and laws of Jesus Christ in obedience, through sacrifice, living the higher laws of the gospel, being temperate and chaste, consecrating all we have and are to do God's work and will to build His kingdom. When we find someone centered in God's covenant work, and who similarly feels for us, our hearts can unite eternally through the new and everlasting covenant of marriage. An ideal temple marriage expresses something like this hypothetical eternal marriage proposal:

"I love you so much that I want to build a family of God with you. I want that family to be centered on Jesus Christ and His gospel. I want to pass on the blessings of the gospel to our children by giving them an heirship to all the truths, covenants, and ordinances of the priesthood. I am willing to commit to you and this by a solemn and

sacred priesthood covenant in God's house. Will you do the work of God with me for eternity so we can become like God, together?"

Admittedly, those exact words aren't the ones most would utter at their rose-petaled engagement proposal, but we recommend that their substance is communicated somewhere in essential conversations around eternal marriage. Their essence must be in us and our spouse if we want to link our hearts in the celestial kingdom of God. Eternal life is *God's life*—it is doing what He does.[17] Exaltation is His work. When we choose to get sealed, we willingly become one and enter into "partnership"[18] with God, doing His work in our own home and family on earth.

THE SEALING COVENANTS

Thus, creating an eternal union between a man and woman of God, to do the work of God, in the ways of God, is central to the temple marriage sealing covenant. Elder Dale G. Renlund taught, "As a man and a woman are sealed, they covenant with God to keep all the commandments related to marriage in the new and everlasting covenant."[19] Understanding important scriptural and prophetic teachings related to the marriage sealing covenant can help us be better prepared to make and keep those covenants.

THE HOLY SEALING

Cleave to Each Other

When Adam and Eve were married in the Garden of Eden by the Lord, it was expressed, "Therefore shall a man leave his father and his mother, and shall cleave unto his wife: and they shall be one flesh" (Genesis 2:24). To "cleave" means to "adhere firmly and closely or loyally and unwaveringly,"[20] like how the Lord tells us to cleave to Him (see Doctrine and Covenants 11:19) or how God cleaves to us (see Jacob 6:5) or Emma Smith was told to "cleave" to her covenants (see Doctrine and Covenants 25:13). The Doctrine and Covenants commands husbands: "Thou shalt *love* thy wife with all thy heart, and shalt *cleave* unto her" (Doctrine and Covenants 42:22; emphasis added). This complete love and cleaving applies equally to the wife toward her husband.[21] It's been said that this command to love our spouse is the only place in scripture where God directs us to love something with all our heart other than Him.[22] *The General Handbook* teaches, "Married couples cleave together by loving and serving each other."[23] One of the greatest ways we show love is through sacrifice (see John 15:13), specifically sacrificing our own selfish desires to serve God and one another in our family.

THE HEARTS

Chaste and Faithful in Family

Cleaving in the context of marriage also suggests the sacredness of sexual intimacy between husband and wife and keeping our individual covenant of chastity. "Cleaving . . . includes total fidelity between husband and wife," the Church explains.[24] The Doctrine and Covenants links cleaving to sexual fidelity when the command to cleave is followed by verses to not "[look] upon [another] woman to lust after her" and "Thou shalt not commit adultery" (Doctrine and Covenants 42:23–24). Cleaving "means there is no emotional intimacy or sexual relations of any kind outside of your marriage, including flirting or dating, and there is no pornography," explained Elder Matthew Carpenter of the Seventy.[25] This includes virtual relationships through technology.[26] Cleaving in total devoted chastity creates the relational environment for complete trust, union, loyalty, safety, and selfless care that is required to establish an eternal covenant family.[27] Our covenant to cleave means we may share in mutual sexual intimacy[28] with our spouse to express love, strengthen connection, and so "that the earth might answer the end of its creation; and that it might be filled with the measure of man" (Doctrine and Covenants 49:16–17). When Adam and Eve were married by God

THE HOLY SEALING

in the Garden of Eden, the scriptures record, "God blessed them, and God said unto them, Be fruitful, and multiply, and replenish the earth" (Genesis 1:28). This wasn't just a command for them in their time, but it "remains in force,"[29] as the Family Proclamation says, as a command for righteous husbands and wives today. We multiply and replenish so that we might have joy in our posterity (see 2 Nephi 2:25) in the day of the Lord.

Coequal Labor and Counsel Together

Our covenant to cleave with our spouse and raise a family of God requires work. We covenant to labor in marriage with one another as equal partners.[30] This pattern of equal marital partnership is exemplified by Adam and Eve.[31] They labored together (Moses 5:1), had children together (v. 2), prayed, worshipped, and received revelation together (vv. 4–5), prophesied together (vv. 10–11), and taught their children together (v. 12). They both were given dominion over the earth (Genesis 1:28; Abraham 4:26) and worked to fulfill that stewardship together. As the ongoing Restoration has continued, the Lord's modern servants have clarified that women and men are equal in receiving revelation, making marital decisions, and leading their families.[32] Modern prophets teach that a husband and wife are equal partners,[33] that there is no president and vice president.[34] There is no ecclesiastic bishop and first counselor model in the marriage.[35] Covenant spouses don't walk ahead or behind each other in governing the family, but lead side by side, without one dominating the other.[36] In working together, we counsel with each other, seeking and valuing the perspective of each partner to make decisions in unity.[37] We speak the truth in love, avoiding contention. We strengthen each other in all our conversations, using Christ-centered communication in both methods and message.[38]

Teaching the Gospel

As we covenant to do the work of God in our marriage, home, and family, we strive to keep His covenants and laws and perpetuate them. To *keep* means to safeguard, to protect, to hold sacred, to prioritize, to cause to live on. As Nephi taught his people, "And we did observe to keep the judgments, and the statutes, and the commandments of the Lord" (2 Nephi 5:10; see also Jacob 3:6; Mosiah 6:6; Doctrine and Covenants 42:78). In our sealing covenants with our spouse, we promise to cause to be taught and continue the everlasting covenant—with its associated teachings, commandments, and ordinances—in our marriage and family (see Mosiah 1:2–8; Doctrine and Covenants 86:10).

THE HOLY SEALING

Living Priesthood Principles

Because we are sealed by the priesthood to do the work of the priesthood (see chapter 2, "The Glory"), we covenant to live our eternal marriage according to priesthood principles. President Dallin H. Oaks taught, "If fathers would magnify their priesthood in their own family, it would further the mission of the Church as much as anything else they might do. Fathers who hold the Melchizedek Priesthood should exercise their authority 'by persuasion, by long-suffering, by gentleness and meekness, and by love unfeigned' (Doctrine and Covenants 121:41). That high standard for the exercise of all priesthood authority is most important in the family."[39] Covenant wives and mothers also exercise priesthood authority[40] in the home in righteousness, as "the heavens are just as open to *women* who are endowed with God's power flowing from their priesthood covenants as they are to men who bear the priesthood," as President Russell M. Nelson has explained.[41]

Agency

Our covenants with God and sealing to another are all based on our agency. There will be no spousal sealing relationships that we don't choose. By their very nature, enduring marriage relationships are voluntary. As President Russell M. Nelson said, God "honors your agency. You are free to choose who you will be—and with whom you will be—in the world to come!"[42] We aren't coerced into sealing corners in the celestial kingdom.[43] Agency is eternally central. Without agency, "there is no existence" (Doctrine and Covenants 93:30), including no existence of a sealed spousal relationship.[44]

With these covenants in mind, as Relief Society General President Jean Bingham asked, "Are we ready? Will we strive to overcome cultural bias and instead embrace divine patterns and practices based on foundational doctrine?"[45] Creating an eternal marriage requires that we look to God and live His celestial covenants in righteousness, and not fall prey to worldly ways. "That which is governed by law is also preserved by law" the Lord revealed, including laws of eternal marriage (Doctrine and Covenants 88:34).

PREPARED FOR THE WORK

Admittedly, for some, reading this about the work of sealing may feel somewhat overwhelming. We love deeply, yes, but we also are conscious of our mortal weakness and failings, particularly in relationships. Remember, however, that God gives high standards to point us where to properly aim, for in striving we can become more than we are at present, and the gospel begs becoming. There will be failings, of course. That is why the foundation of an eternal marriage is and must be on Jesus Christ (see chapter 7, "The Mediator"). It is only through continual repentance, forgiveness, and grace—between God and each other—that the shortcomings of mortal marriage can be repaired and strengthened to endure for eternity.[46] How do we know if our hearts are ready, then, to do this work of eternal marriage and family? Let's look to Abraham, paraphrasing in questions the temple blessings he said he desired in Abraham 1:2:

- Do I desire the exalted family blessings of Adam and Eve?
- Do I want the blessings of priesthood power in my marriage, home, and family?
- Do I want to be a greater follower of righteousness?
- Do I want to be a righteous father or mother?
- Do I seek to establish peace?
- Do I desire to receive more instruction and guidance from heaven?

If yes, then those are signs of a heart that is ready to become a "rightful heir" (Abraham 1:2) of the blessings of the priesthood, sealed through the covenants of eternal marriage. Just as your baptismal covenants prepare you for the endowment, living your endowment covenants prepares you to be sealed with a spouse.[47] Remember, "if ye have desires to serve God ye are called to the work" (Doctrine and Covenants 4:3). That promise isn't limited to missionary preaching. "The work" of God is family-centric, faith-based work. You have desires. You are called. You are ready to embark in this service. "Faith, hope, charity and love, with an eye single to the glory of God glory, qualify [you] for the work" (Doctrine and Covenants 4:5), including the work of eternal marriage.[48] With God, nothing shall be impossible.

CEMENTING THE SEALING

Returning to where we began, there is one last important item of instruction that Melissa and Benjamin Johnson received from their prophetic company that day of May 15, 1843. Joseph sealed them, yes, but he also taught them something more—that they had to cement their sealing in righteousness. "[Joseph] said there was two seals in the Priesthood. The first was that which was placed upon a man and woman when they made the covenant & the other was the seal which alloted to them their particular mansion."[49]

THE HOLY SEALING

Or, as the Doctrine and Covenants says it, through our faithful keeping of covenants, we must be "sealed . . . by the Holy Spirit of promise" (Doctrine and Covenants 132:19). Prophets have taught that this phrase, the "Holy Spirit of Promise," is God's ratification by the Holy Ghost that we have been faithful to our covenant promises.[50] Until then, the blessings are conditional,[51] because all covenants that are not "sealed by the Holy Spirit of promise . . . are of no efficacy, virtue, or force in and after the resurrection from the dead" (Doctrine and Covenants 132:7). Through a temple marriage we have a *promissory* sealing with our spouse, or an eternal opportunity,[52] but it will only be actualized by our faithfulness to the sealing covenant. We retain our spouse's love in eternity by the way we maintain that love in mortality.[53]

Let us be as Abraham, who "against hope believed in hope, that he might become the father of many nations" and "was strong in faith, giving glory to God . . . being fully persuaded that, what he had promised, he was able also to perform" (Romans 4:18, 20–21). With God's grace we can perform this faith-based, family-centric, covenant work of sealing. Like Benjamin and Melissa Johnson, we also take each other's hands in faith to be sealed, and then live our covenants and intertwine our hearts to one another and to God to cement that sealing in eternity. We do so not only for our eternal exaltation but also so that "the promise might be sure to all the seed" (Romans 4:16) and our children might become rightful heirs of exaltation also.

CHAPTER 4

THE HEIRS

A Covenant Lineage

It is November 27, 1832, and W. W. Phelps—a leader of the Church in Missouri—is perplexed.

At hand were some disobedient Church members who had migrated over the summer to Missouri and its city of Zion.[1] They had done so without permission and were unwilling to abide its required covenants, such as living the law of consecration. Should they receive an inheritance[2] of land and have their names recorded among the faithful Saints in the city of God? Picking up his pen over the summer[3] and again in the late fall, Phelps wrote the Prophet Joseph Smith in Ohio, asking counsel on this issue of celestial settlement. Joseph replied in a letter—one that would later have parts canonized—with the revelatory word of the Lord:

THE HEIRS

It is contrary to the will and commandment of God that those who receive not their inheritance by consecration . . . should have their names enrolled with the people of God. Neither is their genealogy to be kept, or to be had where it may be found on any of the records or history of the church. Their names shall not be found, neither the names of the fathers, nor the names of the children written in the book of the law of God, saith the Lord of Hosts. . . . [They] shall not find an inheritance among the saints of the Most High. Therefore, it shall be done unto them as unto the children of the priest, as will be found recorded in the second chapter and sixty-first and second verses of Ezra.[4]

That is a thundering "*therefore*."

For those unfamiliar with these verses in Ezra, this book details thousands of Jews returning to Jerusalem after their long Babylonian exile to rebuild their holy city, including their temple. The priests that had the lawful lineage from Aaron and Levi to act in their temple duties had to prove their priestly lineage down through the generations. But what about those who couldn't trace their familial connection as a descendant heir of the priesthood? Ezra tells us, "And the children of the priests . . . sought their register among those that were reckoned by genealogy, but they were not found: therefore were they, as polluted, put from the priesthood" (Ezra 2:61–62).

If they couldn't prove themselves heirs of the priesthood by lineage descent, they were excluded from it. They would have no priestly inheritance in the city of God in Jerusalem. Over two thousand years later in the New Jerusalem in Missouri, those who wouldn't live celestial laws could not receive an inheritance in the city of God either—nor could their families.

What does this history of a priestly lineage of covenant inheritance have to do with us today and the subject of sealing? Everything.

A COVENANT PRIESTHOOD LINEAGE

In this final dispensation, God is creating a "kingdom of priests" (Exodus 19:6) and a "royal priesthood" (1 Peter 2:9) through the ordinances, power, and blessings of the house of the Lord. In preparing the sisters of the Relief Society for the temple endowment, Joseph Smith told them that he "was going to make of this [Relief] Society a kingdom of Priests"[5] and that the "sisters would come in possession of the privileges, blessings and gifts of the Priesthood"[6] through temple ordinances.[7] Remember, as discussed in chapter 2, priesthood isn't only an ecclesiastical office for men; it is also a covenant order for us all. Like sister*hood* or brother*hood*, priest*hood* is a covenant community of priests. Our ceremonial temple clothing[8] suggests our covenant identity and future as priests or priestesses. In the Old Testament, the only people who were washed and anointed, put on priestly clothes, and entered the holiest room in the temple symbolizing God's presence were prophets, priests, and kings. Today, every worthy Latter-day Saint can do this, male or female. The Lord, through His holy temple, is indeed creating a kingdom of priests and priestesses.

While in the Church it is typical to mention a man's *ecclesiastical* priesthood line of authority, we are not as accustomed to thinking about our *covenant priesthood lineage*. While it is necessary for a man to be able to trace his ecclesiastical Church priesthood office of elder from him to Joseph Smith to Peter, James, and John—and therefore to Jesus—*there seems to be a similar need to establish a covenant lineage for all women and men of God.* Read the scriptures closely, and we see that lineage matters in the covenant (see Genesis 5; 10–11). The New Testament opens its pages with "the generation of Jesus Christ" tracing His lineage down a line to Abraham (see Matthew 1:1–16). Luke traces Jesus's genealogy down a different line but equally back to Abraham, and then from Abraham to Adam (see Luke

THE HOLY SEALING

3:23–38). God commanded Lehi and Sariah's children to go on a long and dangerous mission back to Jerusalem in part to obtain "a genealogy of his fathers" so he could know he was "a descendant of Joseph . . . the son of Jacob" (1 Nephi 5:14). Today, each member of the Church can receive a patriarchal blessing, importantly to declare their lineage connection to Abraham in the house of Israel. Why do we need to know our covenant lineage to be an heir in the kingdom of God?

The Lord promised Abraham that all who received the gospel would become his seed, and therefore potential heirs of the exalted blessings of eternal life (see Abraham 2:10–11). In the same way that a man traces his ecclesiastical priesthood office to Jesus, today all who desire exaltation establish their covenant family lineage to Abraham as an heir of the blessings and covenants of the priesthood. Like how Anthony Sweat was ordained an elder by his father, both Anthony and Cindy Sweat are connected in *the covenant patriarchal lineage* through their respectively sealed parents, who are connected to theirs, seeking to follow a covenant priesthood lineage through our genealogy until we come to Jacob (Israel) who was connected as an heir through Isaac and Rebekah, who was connected as an heir through Abraham and Sarah, who connected through Melchizedek (see Doctrine and Covenants

84:14; Abraham 1:1–3), "who received it through the lineage of his fathers, even till Noah . . . till Enoch . . . to Abel . . . [to] his father Adam, who was the first man" (Doctrine and Covenants 84:14–16) back to God.

Perhaps you're reading this and thinking, "But I'm not sealed to my parents," or, "My covenant lineage stops after a few generations." Because of others' agency and dispensational apostasy, that's true for most all of us—for some sooner and others later. This is part of the reason why we're seeking to link all generations through temple ordinances and sealing for the dead to forge the great "chain" of the priesthood through all dispensations (see chapter 6, "The Offering"). We're trying to establish a royal covenant family lineage for us all. This royal covenant lineage comes as a birthright blessing through temple endowment and marriage sealing—being brought into a lineage of kings and queens, priests and priestesses in Israel. How else can we ever lay claim to a crown without a royal descent? Through temple ordinances we enter in and connect to this royal patriarchal lineage—the exalted family line of God that facilitates its blessings to flow to us as heirs and, through us, on to our children.

THE HOLY SEALING

HEIRS OF THE COVENANT

There is only one general ordinance in the Church where we use the word "heir," and that is in sealing a child to his or her parents in the temple. But that is not the only place the word "heir" is found in the Church. The scriptures are full of it. Paul speaks of being "heirs of God, and joint-heirs with Jesus Christ" (Romans 8:17). The revelations of the Lord to Joseph Smith speak of *heirs*, *lineage*, and *priesthood*. "Therefore, thus saith the Lord unto you, with whom the *priesthood* hath continued through the *lineage* of your fathers— for ye are lawful *heirs*" (Doctrine and Covenants 86:8–9; emphasis added). "Put on the authority of the *priesthood*, which she, Zion, has a right to by *lineage*" (Doctrine and Covenants 113:8; emphasis added). Blessings come "to the inhabitants of Zion, and unto their generations, inasmuch as they become *heirs* according to the laws of the kingdom" (Doctrine and Covenants 70:8; emphasis added). Father Abraham says he "became a *rightful heir, a High Priest*, holding the right belonging to the fathers" (Abraham 1:2; emphasis added). As Abraham's seed and through temple ordinances, we can also become rightful heirs of the blessings of the priesthood through the covenant lineage of our fathers.[9]

Most of us naturally understand the concept of

being an heir. We "inherit" things from our parents, for good and bad: DNA, physical traits, names, material items, language, and more. These things simply come to us, and not to others, by right of birth. It's part of being in the family. In the Lord's kingdom (pause and think about that word, "kingdom") the concept of being an heir continues, only instead of inheriting earthly things, we are "heirs according to the covenant" (Doctrine and Covenants 52:2) through the blessings of the gospel, temple, and sealing power. President Russell M. Nelson taught, "Children born to parents thus married [in the temple] are natural heirs to the blessings of the priesthood," becoming the "posterity of promise."[10]

Children sealed to parents are entitled to the same. Have you ever wondered why we seal children to parents? Particularly if they are going to grow up, be endowed, and get married and sealed to their own spouses? There are various reasons to seal children to parents (see chapter 5, "The Network," for example), but *a central purpose is to establish their covenant lineage as heirs of the blessings of the priesthood.* As faithful heirs of the exalted covenant, through the Savior's grace we can "inherit thrones, kingdoms, principalities, and powers, dominions, all heights and depths . . . exaltation and glory in all things, as hath been sealed upon their heads" (Doctrine and Covenants 132:19). We can become future kings and priests and queens and priestesses in the kingdom of God. Through the temple we become "literal descendants of the chosen seed to whom the promises [are] made," which promises come "down by lineage" (Doctrine and Covenants 107:40–41).

RIGHTFUL AND LAWFUL HEIRS

Unlike earthly monarchies where crown and kingdom can be conferred automatically (or won through corruption or usurpation), covenant crowns are conditional.[11] As Jesus reminded certain Jews who got too caught up in Abrahamic lineage at the expense of holiness, "If ye were Abraham's children, ye would do the works of Abraham" (John 8:39). Meaning can be found in the different scriptural modifiers of being a "lawful heirs" (Doctrine and Covenants 86:9) and a "rightful heir" (Abraham 1:2). One way to interpret these differences is that we become *lawful* heirs by entering the covenant priesthood family of God through the temple and sealing blessings but become *rightful* heirs through keeping our covenants.[12] "Lawful" gives us the opportunity, but "rightful" righteousness secures the blessings. Otherwise, "the axe is laid . . . [and] every tree therefore which bringeth not forth good fruit is hewn down" (Luke 3:9), covenant lineage and Abrahamic birthright notwithstanding.

THE HEIRS

As Joseph Smith wrote from Liberty Jail, unfaithful Saints "shall be severed from the ordinances of mine house" and "they shall not have right to the priesthood, nor their posterity after them from generation to generation" (Doctrine and Covenants 121:19, 21). If someone is "severed" from the ordinances of the temple, they are cut off from the temple and its priesthood blessings, without which they cannot be heirs nor have an increase and are thus "cursed" (see Malachi 4:6). Severed from the patriarchal line, they do not "have the right to the priesthood," nor do their children as heirs. "All thrones and dominions, principalities and powers" shall only be set forth "upon all who have endured valiantly for the gospel of Jesus Christ" (Doctrine and Covenants 121:29).

ALL AS HEIRS

You've likely heard the phrase "born in the covenant" in the Church. The acronym for it is "BIC" and is found on certain Church records next to someone's name. This identifier means that the child's mother and father were sealed in the temple before the baby was born, and therefore the child automatically became an heir of the blessings of Abraham by the act of birth. Once given, that birthright cannot be taken from a covenant child by the divorce or sealing cancellation of the child's parents. Thus, in the Church today, children are not resealed to someone else if their parents' original sealing is canceled and the birth parent seals to a different spouse.[13] Why? Because the child is already in the covenant family of God as a birthright heir.

Those who are not born in the covenant can be sealed to their parents once their parents are endowed and sealed to a spouse, and thus they receive the blessings of being an heir equally, just as if they were born in the covenant. Because of a lack of perfectly clean sealed covenant lines all the way back to Abraham, many are "adopted" into the royal covenant lineage through choosing to accept the gospel covenant by baptism, becoming endowed in the temple, and sealed. Nephi was told that Gentiles (those not of the covenant lineage) who use their agency to choose to "hearken unto the Lamb of God" would be "numbered among the seed of thy father; yea, they shall be numbered among the house of Israel" (1 Nephi 14:1–2). God desires *everyone* to become heirs of the covenant blessings of the patriarchal priesthood[14] so that none are lost or denied opportunity for eternal growth and progression. However, today, many of God's children are covenant disconnected through no fault of their own, limiting potential blessings.

THE HEIRS

BLESSING AND REACHING ALL

There is no simpler truth than "[God] loveth his children" (1 Nephi 11:17). All of them. "He inviteth them all to come unto him and partake of his goodness; and he denieth none that come unto him, black and white, bond and free, male and female . . . all are like unto God, both Jew and Gentile" (2 Nephi 26:33). God desires all to return and receive the highest blessings of exaltation. As of yet, however, too many are kept from the truth because they know not where to find it. They are not yet lawful heirs because there's no knowledge or connection to the covenant family lineage. They are lost, and they don't even know what is eternally available unless they are found.

If they could just be brought into the covenant priesthood lineage, the royal windows of the kingdom could open so there would not be room enough to receive its spiritual blessing. Those covenant heirs would almost naturally learn of God and His great plan and our Savior and redemption through Him. They would be baptized and receive the gift of the Holy Ghost; be blessed by the organization, community, care, and resources of the Church; have opportunities to serve, teach, and lead; be led by living prophets; be enlightened by God's word in the scriptures; and receive

THE HOLY SEALING

divine power, authority, and blessings of priesthood covenants and ordinances: cleansing, healing, strengthening, transforming, miracles, angels, truth, discernment, and more.[15] Full access to God's grace through the Lord's Church and kingdom. What hope! What opportunities! What blessings! "All thy children shall be taught of the Lord; and great shall be the peace of thy children. . . . This is the heritage of the servants of the Lord" (3 Nephi 22:13, 17).

The key is to create heirs of God through bringing each into the covenant priesthood lineage. And for that, we need a network. Not a network of rivers and roads, but of covenant-connected women and men—a kingdom of priests and priestesses who are ready and able to extend the blessings of the royal priesthood to all. We need gatherers to bring the gospel of Jesus Christ to everyone, because "if ye be Christ's, then are ye Abraham's seed, and heirs according to the promise" (Galatians 3:29). It is the central work of the latter days to gather Israel on both sides of the veil[16] through a holy offering to God so that none are lost and all have the opportunity to receive the gospel and the blessings of exaltation. That work is what Joseph Smith called the "welding link," forging from the fire of faith the great network of the eternal priesthood for all.

CHAPTER 5
THE NETWORK
Connecting God's Children

It is January 28, 1844, and Wilford Woodruff is carefully drawing pictures in his journal. Embroidered hearts, to be exact, with twelve smaller hearts and a thirteenth larger heart, connected to one grand heart, all with keys inside of them.

THE HOLY SEALING

Wilford had drawn hearts in his journal before,[1] but never with such potent meaning as this. What could it represent? Hearts often symbolize love, of course, and linked hearts a connection of closeness. The right-facing keys seem to suggest priesthood ordinances, particularly temple ordinances.[2] The text accompanying this drawing helps with its interpretation. On the previous page of the journal, Wilford wrote: "I met with the quorum of the Twelve and others for instruction. . . . The subject of Elijah's coming to seal the hearts of the fathers to the children & &c was spoken of."[3] At the top of the page above the drawing Wilford copied the promise of Elijah found in the book of Malachi: "Seal the hearts of the children to the fathers Malachi IV ch 6 vers." Below it he wrote: "Wilford & Phebe W Woodruff receivd our . . . sealings."[4]

This drawing, however, was not only showing Wilford and Phebe's eternal marriage sealing to each other, but also their connection into a network of kings and priests and queens and priestesses to God.[5] In this case, likely the Twelve Apostles and their wives who had recently received similar ordinances, and perhaps a link to Joseph and Emma Smith—the enlarged thirteenth heart at the head. Who was the largest heart they all connected to? It could be Father Abraham, or Adam, or God, depicting covenant connection into the royal priesthood lineage (see chapter 4, "The Heirs"). Through embroidered hearts and keys, Wilford drew a visual representation of the great chain of the priesthood—the celestial network linking and organizing heaven to do the work of God in eternity. A potent drawing, indeed.

RESTORING THE PRIESTHOOD

If we randomly selected one hundred Latter-day Saints and asked them the question below, how do you think most would respond?

Who restored the priesthood to Joseph Smith?

Most usually say "John the Baptist" or "Peter, James, and John."[6]

While partly correct, those names, however, were not the first given to a seventeen-year-old Joseph Smith in connection to priesthood restoration. In his midnight messages from the angel Moroni, a different name was mentioned. Note who Moroni said would restore the priesthood:

"Behold, I will reveal unto you the Priesthood, by the hand of Elijah the prophet" (Doctrine and Covenants 2:1).

From the beginning, Moroni was pointing Joseph to *Elijah*! Moroni explained Elijah's pinnacle priesthood would "plant in the hearts of the children the promises made to the fathers, and the hearts of the children shall turn to their fathers. If it were not so, the whole earth would be utterly wasted at his coming" (Doctrine and Covenants 2:2–3). This insightful wording reads differently from how Elijah's prophesied coming is phrased in Malachi 4:5–6. Note the emphasized differences below:

Malachi 4:5–6	Doctrine and Covenants 2
I will send you Elijah the prophet	I will *reveal unto you the Priesthood*, by the hand of Elijah the prophet
And he shall turn the heart of the fathers to the children	he shall *plant in the hearts* of the children *the promises made to the fathers*,
lest I come and smite the earth with a curse.	If it were not so, the *whole earth would be utterly wasted* at his coming.

With Moroni's important additions to Malachi's words, a young Joseph Smith learned that Elijah's coming would be centered on "the priesthood," giving "promises" made to "the fathers," so that this earth's purpose would be fulfilled, and not "utterly wasted." As early as 1823, Moroni was directing Joseph Smith to exalted temple blessings centered in family and sealing.[7]

ELIJAH'S ENCOMPASSING KEYS

Thirteen years later, on April 3, 1836, in the Kirtland Temple, the angels Moses and Elias—and finally at last, Elijah!—appeared to Joseph Smith and Oliver Cowdery (see Doctrine and Covenants 110:11–16). These angels gave them essential priesthood keys to gather and connect all of covenant Israel together (Moses), endow the exalted blessings of the dispensation of the gospel of Abraham (Elias), and seal them through the new and everlasting covenant of marriage (Elijah). This day changed everything.

Elijah's priesthood keys enabled *all* exalting temple work to be done, including endowments and sealings.[8] The Prophet Joseph Smith taught, "Why send Elijah [?] because he holds the keys of the Authority to administer in all the ordinances of the priesthood."[9] At another time, the Prophet Joseph taught, "The spirit power & calling of Elijah is that ye have power to hold the keys of the revelations ordinances, oracles powers & endowments of the fulness of the Melchezedek Priesthood & of the kingdom of God on the Earth

THE HOLY SEALING

& to receive, obtain & perform all the ordinances belonging to the kingdom of God."[10]

We often simplify Elijah's restored keys as the "sealing power"—the power to bind on earth and in heaven. That's accurate, but it is more than that. Sealing keys validate all the ordinances of exaltation—including temple work for the dead.[11] With these keys restored, we can bring the scattered and lost family of God together, through the Savior, restoring them to their Heavenly Parents and to each other, roots and branch. We can link ourselves and this last dispensation with our progenitors and prior dispensations. We can create what Joseph called the great "chain" of the priesthood.

THE GREAT CHAIN

In the last culminating years of his life and ministry, Joseph Smith labored diligently to get the temple ordinances and keys of sealing implemented in the Church. In a September 1842 letter, now canonized in Doctrine and Covenants 128, the Prophet wrote pressingly about our ancestors and saving us and them through exercising Elijah's keys: "Let me assure you that these are principles in relation to the dead and the living that cannot be lightly passed over, as pertaining to our salvation. For their salvation is necessary and essential to our salvation" (Doctrine and Covenants

128:15). Citing Elijah's priesthood and how it will turn our hearts to our ancestors and the temple, the Prophet continued: "The earth will be smitten with a curse unless there is a welding link of some kind or other between the fathers and the children. . . . For it is necessary in the ushering in of the dispensation of the fulness of times . . . that a whole and complete and perfect union, and welding together of dispensations, and keys, and powers, and glories should take place, and be revealed from the days of Adam even to the present time" (Doctrine and Covenants 128:18).

This "union" or "welding link" through sealing links us to our families, and our families to past families, all the way back to Adam and Eve, in a royal priesthood lineage. Joseph taught: "Herein is the chain that binds the hearts of the fathers to the children, & the children to the Fathers which fulfills the mission of Elijah & I would to God that this temple was now done that we might go into it & go to work & improve our time & make use of the seals while they are on earth."[12] Maybe part of the reason Joseph felt this sense of urgency is because of Moroni's warning that without this continuation of priesthood, the earth's purpose would be frustrated, unfilled, or "cursed."

If eternal priesthood is familial (see chapter 2, "The Glory"), then we need our families, and they need us. Remember, heaven is relational and priesthood is parental. None of us can be perfected or exalted without one another. But it isn't just connecting us to our spouse and children, or us to our ancestors. As discussed in the last chapter, this work seeks to connect us to our families—spouse, posterity, and ancestry—until we can connect into the royal priesthood lineage of God in dispensations past so that we all can become rightful heirs of exaltation. Thus, there is a *third* group Joseph discusses:

"For we without them cannot be made perfect; neither can they without us be made perfect. *Neither can they nor we be made perfect without those who have died in the gospel also*" (Doctrine and Covenants 128:18; emphasis added). "We" (the living) and "they" (our dead) also need "those who have died in the gospel" (righteous Saints from the past). The living, the dead, and the righteous Saints on the other side of mortality, all linked and connected into a great chain of temple priests and priestesses.[13] We're trying to connect into the power of a celestial network of heavenly Saints. Why?

THE GREAT NETWORK

You've likely flown somewhere. Although modern airline travel can sometimes be taxing, it really is

THE NETWORK

amazing. In the morning you are in New York, and after sitting in a chair watching free movies while sipping a soft drink, by afternoon you're in southern California. But maybe you don't want to go to California. Maybe you need to go from JFK airport to Boise. Good luck finding enough New Yorkers to fill a direct flight to Idaho! But no worries: there's a *network*. There's an organized system of airlines and airports that are linked to get you most anywhere you need to be through available *connections*, as illustrated.

At times, connecting flights are seen negatively, but they are a marvelous solution to a major problem. Without connections, we wouldn't be able to travel

THE HOLY SEALING

everywhere in the world from wherever we live. We would be severely limited. It's the great web of regional carriers connecting to major national and international airports that makes it all possible. There's power in pathways of connection. And all it takes is one or two to open things up for all.

Take a look at this illustration below. As they are, these three groups of letters are limited to their own immediate connections.

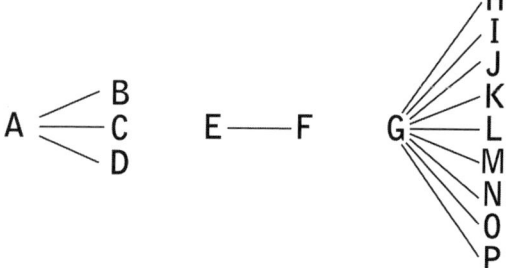

P has no access to D. However, if we just make *two* connections through them, then all these letters are suddenly linked to each other:

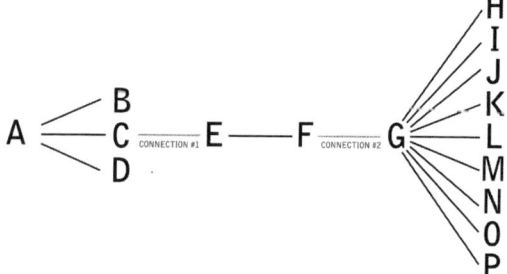

For example, P can get to D like this:

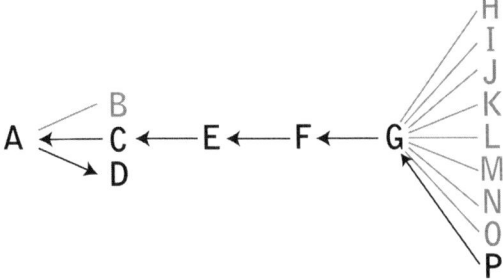

Why do we want P to connect with D? Because D has something that P needs. In the world, *who* you know is sometimes just as important as *what* you know. Think of how many job opportunities have been given because the applicant knows someone who knows someone. It's good connections that open opportunities otherwise unavailable. Humans are constantly creating connective networks to facilitate the flow of power—water, interstate highways, cellular service, internet, social media, electricity, gas. Connections open and facilitate resources, information, pathways, and opportunities that otherwise wouldn't exist independently. *Networks* are the key, temporally and also spiritually.

In the same way that there are enabling powers through mortal networks, there is eternal power through a heavenly network. As shown in Wilford's

THE HOLY SEALING

drawing, there is a heavenly network of holy people we become connected with through the ordinances of the holy temple, the covenants of Abraham, and Elijah's keys. The prayer circle[14] in the temple seems to suggest this truth. The network of sealing connects us to Saints on both sides of the veil. Through the priesthood we are promised the ministering of angels (see Doctrine and Covenants 13:1; 107:20), and prophets have taught that angels who come to our aid may at times be of our own departed ancestry.[15] Now, think if the ministering angels were not only departed immediate family members, but celestial souls over the centuries who see us as theirs. What if Lehi and Sariah, Isaac and Rebekah, Abraham and Sarah, and Adam and Eve were our family? Oh, wait, they are! Through sealing we are brought into their covenant family lines as heirs and thus inheritors of their blessings. A declaration of lineage in a patriarchal blessing gives revelatory insight into divine network connections and blessings. Like an eternal ward family watching out for and ministering to one another, through sealing links members of the exalted "Church of the Firstborn" can have care over us, assist us, and commune with us (see Doctrine and Covenants 107:19). Like letters P and D above, "those who have died in the gospel" are connected to and through us to aid for eternity, bringing priesthood power to all the familial covenant heirs of God. "The heavenly priesthood will unite with the earthly," the Prophet Joseph taught, "to bring about those great purposes," adding, "the Heavenly Priesthood are not idle spectators."[16]

THE ORGANIZATION OF HEAVEN

We were once teaching about this great chain of the priesthood and its potential blessings, and afterward an adult Church member said something like: "Well, it doesn't really matter in the end if we are all sealed together, so long as I am connected to Christ, right?"

Of course, faith in and covenant connection through Christ is the only way, we emphasized (see John 14:6). There's no other means than by His redeeming merits, mercy, and grace (see 2 Nephi 2:8). However, we asked, "How do you see the blessings of the Savior's gospel being extended to everyone? How will we assist to gather in all who are lost? What's the organized means in the spirit world or Millennium to facilitate this?"

This person said, "I've never stopped to think that heaven is *organized*."

"Well," we said with a smile, "it is."

While some details of the spirit world and how the institutional Church operates in the eternal world are not fully revealed,[17] the organization of families appears to be central. The network of heaven doesn't run through wires, cables, or pipes but through husbands, wives, and children connected by the keys and power of the priesthood. "Heaven is organized by families," the Church has taught.[18] Just like how with ecclesiastical priesthood authority Church leaders create new "units" (stakes, wards, districts, branches) to govern and order the global Church, the temple ordinance of eternal marriage and sealing creates a new priesthood family "unit" to govern and order families on earth and in heaven.[19] Indeed, this family unit and priesthood order will likely one day outlive the organization of the ecclesiastical Church.[20] God's house is a house or order, not of chaos, and that order is the eternal family priesthood order.

ETERNAL REACHING MINISTRY

This eternal family priesthood order is organized to bring up souls to God. Our mortal ministering efforts within our families and with other Saints in the network of the Church prepare us to expand our participation in God's work in the network of the eternities. Thus, sealing children to parents seems less about future heavenly living arrangements and more centered in heavenly loving agreements; less about hanging out together and more about reaching out forever. *Being sealed suggests an organization of eternal ministry through loving family ties.*

President Lorenzo Snow taught: "Think of the

promises that are made to you in the beautiful and glorious ceremony that is used in the marriage covenant in the temple. When two Latter-day Saints are united together in marriage, promises are made to them concerning their offspring, that reach from eternity to eternity. They are promised that they shall have the power and the right to govern . . . administering life, exaltation, and glory, worlds without end."[21]

Now we can better see why Wilford drew multiple linked hearts in his journal. Now we may be beginning to better understand why Elijah's keys were pinnacle to the restored priesthood and why Moroni pointed Joseph's young mind toward that moment. Now we can comprehend why Joseph Smith said: "How shall God come to the rescue of this generation? He shall send Elijah . . . and he shall reveal the covenants to seal the hearts of the fathers to the children, and the children to the fathers."[22] Through this patriarchal order of the priesthood, families are eternally connected into a celestial ministering network of Saints across dispensations as they help bring about God's work and glory, extending the blessings of the fulness of the gospel of Jesus Christ to all so that none are lost. Finding and connecting the entire human family to God is the work of the last days, and our great offering to God.

CHAPTER 6

THE OFFERING

None Are Lost

It is January 15, 1847, and Elder Orson Hyde of the Quorum of the Twelve Apostles is saying farewell to the Saints in England.

Orson was ready to rejoin the American "saints in the wilderness," but he hoped "the day is not far distant when the Saints in England will follow us, not only to the American wilderness, but even to the celestial courts on high." Elder Hyde wrote to them as "ye sons and daughters of Zion's King" and promised them one day, "the scepter shall be put into your hands, and crowns upon your heads."[1] Before leaving them, as editor of the *Millennial Star*, he printed what he called "A Diagram of the Kingdom of God." Take a look at it below:

THE OFFERING

A DIAGRAM OF THE KINGDOM OF GOD.

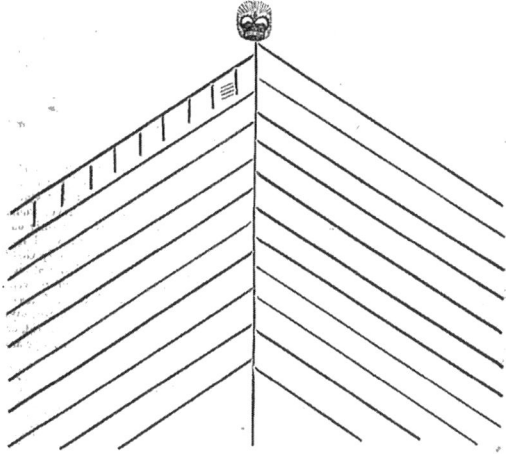

This is not your everyday illustration of heaven. What is going on in this diagram? The top icon is not an image of a person with white eyes and teeth. It is a *king's crown*, fashioned like the crown of England, shining in glory. What are the lines connecting to it, and to one another? Orson Hyde explained:

> The above diagram shows the order and unity of the kingdom of God. The eternal Father sits at the head, crowned King of kings and Lord of lords. Wherever the other lines meet, there sits a king and a priest unto God, bearing rule, authority, and dominion under the Father. He is one with the Father, because his kingdom is

> joined to his Father's and becomes part of it. . . .
> These have received their washings and anointings in the temple of God. . . . They have been chosen, ordained, and anointed kings and priests, to reign as such in the resurrection of the just.[2]

Orson seemed to be drawing his version of the great network of heaven—Saints sealed to one another through the priesthood as heirs of God receiving a fulness of His blessings. However, the drawing is limited and visually incomplete. For example, it doesn't visualize and account for the central role of women as co-equal queens and priestesses. Thus, perhaps rather than a hierarchical structure, you see it more circular as a family "fan chart," like on FamilySearch. We personally visualize the great network like a crosscut of a huge tree, with thousands of lines connecting to one another and from dispensational ring to ring with myriads of possible routes back to the center. In the previous chapter, Wilford Woodruff drew it as linked hearts. But it's less about how it's visualized and more about expressing a compelling divine desire: Everyone can and must be linked into the ordered family and kingdom of God. Through our Savior and His holy priesthood, none are to be lost.

In His great Intercessory Prayer, our Lord prayed:

"While I was with them in the world, I kept them in thy name: those that thou gavest me I have kept, and none of them is lost" (John 17:12; see also John 6:39; 18:9). He was speaking of His Apostles, in context, but prophets have taught that this pastoral love from the Great Shepherd extends to all covenant lambs. President Russell M. Nelson taught, "Once you and I have made a covenant with God, our relationship with Him becomes much closer than before our covenant. Now we are bound together. Because of our covenant with God, He will never tire in His efforts to help us, and we will never exhaust His merciful patience with us. . . . And should [any] stray, He will help them find their way back to Him."[3] Many in the covenant family of Abraham have strayed. Israel is scattered. Branches are cut off. Currently, many *are* lost. How do we gather them in? That's where we come in. That is the work of the last dispensation and our great offering to God through His holy temple and the sealing work therein.

THE GREAT OFFERING

Related to what Moroni taught Joseph Smith about Elijah is the prophecy that God will "purify the sons of Levi, and purge them as gold and silver, that they may offer unto the Lord an offering in righteousness" (Malachi 3:3). The "sons of Levi" in the

THE HOLY SEALING

Old Testament were the chosen priestly lineage to do the work of the temple. The "offerings" to God were mostly sacrificial animals, grain, and incense.[4] But that was then. How can this prophecy apply today? Who is modern Levi, and what is the offering?

Today, the sons of Levi are God's covenant men and women—the seed of Abraham—who "offer an acceptable offering and sacrifice in the house of the Lord" (Doctrine and Covenants 84:31; see also vv. 32–34). They are modern Saints—you and I—serving in the Lord's temples. Instead of offering up animals, we offer *ourselves.* We sacrifice and consecrate our time to bring names and perform essential ordinances in behalf of beloved family, deceased relatives, and the family of God. Why? Because our hearts are filled with the love of God and His children. Through the priesthood restored by Elijah, we seal them up as heirs of the covenant—one by one—into the great network and family of God. *Forging the chain of the priesthood and great covenant network of sealed souls in Christ is our great offering to God.*

Motivated by love, we vicariously do for others what the dead can't do for themselves, performing necessary ordinances in their behalf that open the door of salvation. This is how we become "saviors on Mount Zion."[5] Joseph Smith taught:

THE OFFERING

> But how are [the Saints] to become Saviors on Mount Zion [?] by building their temples erecting their Baptismal fonts & going forth & receiving all the ordinances, Baptisms, confirmations, washings anointings ordinations, & sealing powers upon our heads in behalf of all our Progenitors who are dead & redeem them that they may come forth in the first resurrection & be exhalted to thrones of glory with us, & herein is the chain that binds the hearts of the fathers to the children, & the children to the Fathers which fulfills the mission of Elijah.[6]

This is our "offering in righteousness" as modern sons and daughters of Levi. The Prophet Joseph gave us this interpretation of our work and offering: "Let us . . . as Latter-day Saints, offer unto the Lord an offering in righteousness; and let us present in his holy temple, when it is finished, a book containing the records of our dead" (Doctrine and Covenants 128:24).

This book with the records of the ordinances performed in behalf of God's children—connecting them to Christ, one another, and the broader family of God—represents the offering. The offering creates the network; the network facilitates the teaching and reaching; and the teaching and reaching ensure none are lost. The great covenant priesthood network of heaven, like a welding link, will reach out to and seek to forge together in Christ every soul—living and dead, past, present, and future—who desires to know, accept, and live the fulness of the gospel. This is the great work of the last days.[7] Is it not glorious?

NONE ARE LOST

The marvelous Book of Mormon reminds us that "[God] loveth his children" (1 Nephi 11:17). All of them. Everyone will be invited to "partake of his goodness" and "all men are privileged . . . and none are forbidden" because "all are alike" unto Him, and He "denieth none that come unto him" (2 Nephi 26:28, 33). All will be invited to be included or restored back into the covenant family of God as heirs through the great chain of the priesthood, organized by families, because each soul of the covenant lineage is remembered by God.[8]

If we want physical, tangible evidence that God remembers His covenant children, just study closely the Book of Mormon. In case we've missed it, that is crucial to the whole story and message: God reaching out to a family and their wayward children "that they may know the covenants of the Lord, that they are not cast off forever" (Title Page of the Book of Mormon). Indeed, God reaches out to certain people *because of the covenants, desires, and actions of their righteous parents.*

At His personal appearance and ministry to the Book of Mormon people, the Lord expressed this covenant reaching and remembering thus:

> Behold, ye are the children of the prophets; and ye are of the house of Israel; and ye are of the covenant which the Father made with your fathers. . . . The Father having raised me up unto you first, and sent me to bless you in turning away every one of you from his iniquities; and this because ye are the children of the covenant. (3 Nephi 20:25–26)

When we read these scriptures, let's not read them like they're talking about people in a galaxy far, far away. Let's liken them to ourselves, and our families, that we may have the same hope (see 1 Nephi 19:23–24). We and our children *are* covenant Israel, or can be through the ordinances of the priesthood and house of the Lord. So, verses like the following are about *our* covenant-connected and sealed ones also:

"How merciful is our God unto us, for he remembereth the house of Israel, both roots and branches; and he stretches forth his hands unto them all the day long" (Jacob 6:4).

THE HOLY SEALING

"I am God, and . . . covenanted with Abraham that I would remember his seed forever" (2 Nephi 29:14).

"The Lord hath said unto me, I will preserve thy seed forever" (2 Nephi 3:16).

"And also, that I may remember the promises which I have made unto thee . . . that I would remember your seed" (2 Nephi 29:2).

"That the promise may be fulfilled unto Joseph, that his seed should never perish as long as the earth should stand" (2 Nephi 25:21).

"They shall be gathered in from their long dispersion. . . . And now behold, the Lord remembereth all them who have been broken off" (2 Nephi 10:8, 22).

"To be remembered in the covenants of the Lord that the Messiah should be made manifest unto them in the latter days, in the spirit of power, unto the bringing of them out of darkness unto light" (2 Nephi 3:5).

"As it has been shown unto me that many of our children shall perish in the flesh because of unbelief, nevertheless, God will be merciful unto many; and our children shall be restored, that they may come to that which will give them the true knowledge of their Redeemer" (2 Nephi 10:2).

Before we read the allegory of the olive tree given by the prophet Jacob in Jacob 5, we first need to look at the question he was addressing in Jacob 4. The question was, "How is it possible that these, after having rejected the sure foundation, can ever build upon it, that it may become the head of their corner? . . . I will unfold this mystery unto you" (Jacob 4:17–18). For children of the covenant, Jacob 5 can be applied to *our* individual families. The tree is us and our sealed ones in the broader vineyard of the Lord's eternal covenant family.[9] The tree may decay and lose its natural fruit for a time, but the servants of the Lord—lineage in the patriarchal order—will continue to work for and with the Lord to spiritually prune, graft, dig, and nourish it. By the Lord's grace and priesthood power, He will say, "I have preserved the natural fruit, that it is good, *even like as it was in the beginning*" (Jacob 5:75; emphasis added). Covenant family trees will not be lost.

This covenant reaching through the great network to heirs of the priesthood has been repeatedly promised by prophets (see appendix, "Promises to Posterity"). Of course, moral agency is central and eternal. Nobody will be forced into heaven, and any heir can reject their spiritual birthright (just read the story of Esau). But covenant promises play the millennial long game, and the pull of priesthood tugs on both sides of the veil.[10] Through sealing promises and power, it seems we will continue to minister to our posterity—to love them, serve, support, encourage, bless, teach, guide, lead, nurture, and council with them[11]—bringing forth and producing children who choose to be saved or exalted in the celestial kingdom of God.

Hopefully, this doctrine of covenant priesthood sealing power distills upon our souls as the dews from heaven. Like all priesthood, this parental power comes by way of covenant parents' persuasion, long-suffering, gentleness, meekness, and love unfeigned (see Doctrine and Covenants 121:41–46). Priesthood power is not like worldly power. Priesthood is not power *over*, but power *through*.[12] As we act in accordance with these and other principles of the priesthood, our children will eventually, without compulsory means, turn to God and claim their birthright blessings as children of Abraham and heirs of the priesthood.

A COVENANT RESPONSIBILITY

Until we can create this welding link to and for all, it seems we cannot consider "the priesthood" fully restored. It is the work of the last days, and specifically our privilege and responsibility as covenant Saints in it, to make this great offering to our God. The covenant has been renewed and confirmed upon us for the sake of the whole world (see Doctrine and Covenants 84:48). As D. Todd Christofferson said, "The commitment to aid one another across the veil can be classified as a covenant promise. . . . It is how the covenant promises given to Abraham are realized."[13] It is our covenant responsibility as the Lord's servants to extend these great blessings to others,[14] including the dead. The scriptures say that this communal covenant outreach for and in behalf of those on the other side of the veil is "necessary and essential" to our own salvation (Doctrine and Covenants 128:15). Indeed, this redemptive offering was God's will from the start, "prepared before the foundation of the world, for the salvation of the dead who should die without a knowledge of the gospel" (Doctrine and Covenants 128:5; see also Doctrine and Covenants 124:33).

The call to seek out our ancestors and reach all of the human family can seem daunting. However, because of compounding population rates, it's estimated that over 90 percent of all of humanity has been born on earth since Elijah restored the sealing keys.[15] Incredible technology has emerged to facilitate and hasten vicarious temple work.[16] This offering can only be done in the Lord's holy house under the priesthood keys of His authorized servants (see Doctrine and Covenants 124:29–34). However, we are immensely blessed to live in a time when temples are dotting the earth at unprecedented rates,[17] compounding our ability to make the latter-day offering. It will take the millennial era to complete this work, surely, but it is hastening with remarkable resources and at rapidly accelerating rates as we approach the Lord's return.

JOY AND REJOICING

We all can participate and help with this great offering—a record of each name of God's children and every necessary ordinance done in their behalf—sealing and linking together all of God's children. This is the greatest spiritual work on earth.[18] This is the gathering of Israel. The sealing ordinances are how the great network is organized and facilitated so that through loving family ties, the restored gospel of Jesus Christ extends to all. These connections allow us greater access to knowledge, blessings, and priesthood power than if we were to operate independently. It makes the salvation and exaltation of the human family possible, an eternal family ministering organization through and to posterity so that "none of them is lost" (John 17:12). That's likely why the prophet Joseph asked and exclaimed:

> Shall we not go on in so great a cause? . . . Let your hearts rejoice, and be exceedingly glad. Let the earth break forth into singing. Let the dead

THE OFFERING

speak forth anthems of eternal praise to the King Immanuel, who hath ordained, before the world was, that which would enable us to redeem them. . . . And again I say, how glorious is the voice we hear from heaven, proclaiming in our ears, glory, and salvation, and honor, and immortality, and eternal life; kingdoms, principalities, and powers!" (Doctrine and Covenants 128:22–23)

This rejoicing of our hearts comes by participating with the Lord in His redeeming work of salvation and exaltation. The joy that comes from bringing but one soul to Him is great, let alone the many souls that the temple offering and priesthood network facilitate. The worth of souls is indeed great in God's sight (see Doctrine and Covenants 18:10, 13–16), and the joy of finding symbolic lost coins, sheep, and prodigal souls incalculable (see Luke 15). Because of the Lord's goodness and grace, exalting opportunities will be made available through the Great Network and latter-day offering to all who choose to make and keep covenants, regardless of limitations on earth. But this mediating for our families and God's children—past, present, and future—is possible only because of the Mediator of us all, infinite and eternal.

CHAPTER 7

THE MEDIATOR
Our Intended Condition

It is the first weekend of April, around AD 30, about 3:00 p.m.,[1] and just outside of Jerusalem's walls, the God of heaven and earth suffers. Nailed to a cruel cross, our Lord is slain for the sins of the world. Masses of Passover pilgrims pass by the suffering Son, watching Him torturously die. Some weep. Some mock. Some turn away. Some are disinterested. He suffers. He thirsts. "Why hast thou forsaken me?" He asks. His body slumps. He who breathed the breath of life takes His last breath of life, and the Son of God dies.

Words escape the horror of Jesus's death, but to believers, this voluntary sacrifice is our Lord's greatest act of love (see John 15:13). The axis of eternity hinges upon Christ's death to atone for this fallen world.

Without it, everything—including us—is lost forever. With it, however, we can all live forever.

This redeeming truth also applies to families. Perhaps as you've read the preceding chapters, a wave of worry has washed over you. While we've been writing thoughts expounding the dream, the hearts, the priesthood, the heirs, the network, and the offering, you may have been fighting thoughts about how this does or doesn't work for your particular life or family. Your situation is complicated. Your marriage isn't easy. Covenant relationships with your children are tenuous, or with no heirs apparent. *And if only we knew your parents*, you say! The truth is that the pains and problems of mortality creep through the cracks of *every* covenant home. Even if our present family situation feels close to heaven and abounds in blessed love, when it comes to sealing roots and branches through our ancestors and children, nobody has a perfectly formed family tree. All of us have disconnected lines because of divorce, death, remarriage, singleness, or unfaithfulness. In not a few generations, the great network of sealing can look more like a mess of knotted cables, hopelessly tangled, disconnected, or broken. In a book on eternal sealing that is confounded by mortal situations, what is to be done? There is only one answer, of course. It is our Savior, Jesus the Christ.

THE HOLY SEALING

"And for this cause he is the mediator of the new testament . . . [that] they which are called might receive the promise of eternal inheritance" (Hebrews 9:15).

REDEEMING RELATIONSHIPS

While we are accustomed to speaking about the Lord's grace saving individuals, through the Lord's redemption, *families* will also be redeemed eternally. The reality is that without Jesus Christ, there is no eternal family. Through Him, however, we can be bound to our immediate family in God and ultimately restored to the broader covenant family of God. Jesus Christ is "the mediator of the new covenant" (Doctrine and Covenants 76:69), including the holy covenants of sealing and the promised blessings of Abraham.[2] Through His atoning grace we can be cleansed, healed, restored, strengthened, and transformed, and so can our families. Jesus Christ alone is able to make us holy (see Doctrine and Covenants 60:7) and endow us with priesthood power and capacity to abide in the presence of God, lovingly linked with our loved ones.

Some seem to naively think the power of human love or desire is enough to enable eternal family and exalted progression, as if some cosmic force of feeling can conquer sin and death and bind us together forever in the presence of God. That, however, is merely wishful thinking, as a modern prophet once said.[3] We need a Mediator to overcome our mortal frailties and failures. For our relationships to be fit for eternity, we must build upon the gospel of Jesus Christ. We must find hope in His divine promises, particularly that His "grace is sufficient" (Doctrine and Covenants 17:8) to mediate and create eternal ties that bind us as one.

FOUNDING AND BUILDING RELATIONSHIPS

Helaman tells us, "Remember, remember that it is upon the rock of our Redeemer who is Christ" that we can build our only "sure foundation" (Helaman 5:12). That double reminder is true for us individually and for our eternal marriage and family. This truth is emphasized in the temple. The Savior is the center of the sealing ceremony. We kneel over an altar of sacrifice that symbolizes our Lord's divine offering,[4] expressing through humble bended knees that we will base our marriage upon His teachings and Atonement. We take each other's hand over that altar, signifying that our very eternal connection to one another is only possible because of His suffering, death, and power of resurrection. When we are sealed in a temple to our spouse or children, through the place, clothing, signs, symbols, setting, and words, we set Jesus Christ as the center of our life, marriage, and family.

THE HOLY SEALING

As we leave the temple and reenter the world, we take and wear a sacred symbol of Christ with us—the garment of the holy priesthood[5]—reminding us of holy covenants and teachings to govern our lives. Practically, the Lord—the Prince of Peace—lays the path for peaceful relationships: turning the other cheek, forgiving others their trespasses, selflessly serving one another, being meek and humble. Striving to live by priesthood principles such as gentleness, temperance (self-control), kindness, patience, and love enable relationships to be healthy, trusting, and enduring. Relationships can't thrive on sin, pride, vanity, or compulsion (see Doctrine and Covenants 121:37–42). The endowment covenants give us divine laws to follow for our family's peace and progression: obedience, sacrifice, the gospel, chastity, and consecration. Establishing our families on the covenant teachings of Jesus Christ helps enable our family relationships to endure through eternity.

HEALING RELATIONSHIPS

Of course, unfortunately, in our families we don't always follow the Savior's teachings. We are mere mortals, after all. Through a combination of human weakness that can add up over time or deliberate sins of more egregious errors, we hurt ourselves and others, harming

THE MEDIATOR

relationships. We've left metaphorical Jerusalem and descended down toward Jericho, falling among relational thieves that leave love wounded. We need the divine good Samaritan to pour oil upon our homes and bind up our familial hurts. All our marriages and families need atoning healing, to varying degrees.

The ultimate definition of the word *Atonement* means to reconcile or to restore to harmony.[6] If we break the word down into three parts (at-one-ment), we can more clearly understand what is meant by the idea: to take that which was out of harmony and make it "at one" again or put in its proper, rightful, intended condition. Although we are imperfect mortals here on earth, through Christ's divine sacrifice, by obedience to the laws and ordinances of His gospel, we can be reconciled, redeemed, or restored "at-one" again with our perfect immortal Father in Heaven. This is the essence of the gospel, the "good news."

This divine power of reconciliation also applies to our fallen mortal relationships, allowing them to be divinely mediated and made whole through Christ. President Boyd K. Packer taught, "Restoring what you cannot restore, healing the wound you cannot heal, fixing that which you broke and you cannot fix is the very purpose of the atonement of Christ."[7] If Paul can convert, Alma the younger repent, and Lamanites bury weapons of war, so too can the Lord mediate and convert family sin, hatred, disconnect, and dysfunction. If Christ can heal eyes and ears and legs then He can also heal loneliness, hurt, and betrayal.[8] Do you think your relationship or family is too far fallen? Maybe on your own and now, yes. Or with that particular person, perhaps. But with the miraculous millennial mixture of God, grace, agency, and time, all things are possible. The Lord once promised, "And after their temptations, and much tribulation, behold, I, the Lord, will feel after them, and if they harden not their hearts, and stiffen not their necks against me, they shall be converted, and I will heal them" (Doctrine and Covenants 112:13).

Similar promises apply also for us. Elder Gerrit W. Gong said, "Our Savior is our Mediator with God, but He also helps bring us to ourselves and each other as we come to Him. Especially when hurt and pain are deep, repairing our relationships and healing our hearts is hard, perhaps impossible for us on our own. But heaven can give us strength and wisdom beyond our own to know when to hold on and how to let go."[9]

Maybe you or your loved one is currently unable to abide in a particular family relationship, for very good and justifiable reasons. But let's never forget that if we will let Him, the Lord can change us and others. Like water washing over rocks in rivers, timeless grace can polish any rough soul over millennia and epochs of agency. Speaking of inheritors of the celestial glory who are "priests and kings [and queens and priestesses] who have received of [God's] fulness," the scriptures remind us, "These are they who are just men made perfect through Jesus the mediator of the new covenant" (Doctrine and Covenants 76:56, 69). Good people ("just"), but also *just* (or regular) people who are made perfect in Christ. Or as Moroni said it, "Come unto Christ, and be perfected in him . . . that by his grace ye may be perfect in Christ" (Moroni 10:32). Thus, "I would that ye should look to the great Mediator" (2 Nephi 2:28) Lehi exhorted members of his own family, and we should do the same for us and ours.

RESTORING RELATIONSHIPS

Mediating and atoning also involve divine *restoring*. "The Restoration" isn't only about reestablishing the authorized Church, but it is about Christ putting all things in their intended heavenly condition. The Lord will remake this earth into heaven, where God's will is perfectly done (see Matthew 6:10). The work of the Restoration is to restore things to their proper order—to take things that are imperfect and broken and make them whole. In Alma chapter 40, Alma uses the Resurrection as a shadow to help us understand the broader work of the restoration of all things.[10] Alma says of the body that "every limb and joint shall be restored . . . all things shall be restored to their proper and perfect frame" (Alma 40:23).

The Lord will conquer all the effects of the fallen world, including error, inequity, injustice, unfairness, and lost or denied opportunities. Whether in this life or the next, Christ will repay, reinstate, renew, refresh, or return any blessing that was lost, denied, or taken in this life. He will perfectly restore, rectify, redeem, and recompense any injustice or undue suffering that was a result of our mortal experience. The central feature of the Atonement of Jesus Christ is to perfectly right every mortal wrong.[11] This truth provides a type for restoring the sealed family of God. Speaking to mothers whose young children had died, the Prophet Joseph Smith once said, "All your losses will be made up to you in the resurrection, provided you continue faithful. By the vision of the Almighty I have seen it."[12] For the covenant faithful, these restoring promises include "eternal marriage, children, and all other blessings of an eternal family."[13]

The Lord's work of restoration also includes restoring our great Latter-day offering in the temple to seal up the whole human family to God and each other. Are we making mistakes in these millions of ordinance offerings for the dead? Of course. Should we not have sealed Grandma to Grandpa, given their tenuous situation? Only they can say (and they aren't here). Did we miss connecting a child into their family covenant, or seal someone to the wrong parent? Perhaps, unfortunately. Will some on the other side reject the relationship we vicariously sealed here? Maybe, as agency is eternal. The sealing work for the living and dead in the Lord's house, while inspiring, is imperfect. Our offering is but loaves and fishes, but nonetheless we offer all that we can and we have faith that the Savior's grace will multiply the goodness and reconcile any imperfections in it. Like apprentice artists who learn as they lay the necessary groundwork on a painting, the Master completes and finishes it off with his unique gifts. The family organization of heaven will be perfected and restored to its proper and perfect condition. Remember, Brigham saw it. Trust the Lord Omnipotent. His grace is sufficient.

CURRENT RELATIONSHIPS

So, after all that's been said in these chapters, what can we do *right now* related to sealing? Regardless of current familial situations, there are truths we've sought to articulate in this book that can lead to actionable applications for us all. The following are some invitations related to the holy sealing we can each implement now:

1. ***Come unto Christ.*** As the Savior is the center of sealing, He must be the center of our individual lives. Let's build the foundation of our life upon Him. Let's learn of Him, listen to His words, and walk in the meekness of His Spirit (see Doctrine and Covenants 19:23). Let's act with faith in His ways, continually repent and realign our lives with His will, renew and deepen our covenant commitment to Him through His ordinances, and receive the Holy Spirit. Always. Let's talk of Him, preach of Him, and rejoice in His divinity, Atonement, and grace, no matter our current marital or family circumstance. We've been taught and promised that we can have joy in Christ no matter the circumstances of our lives.[14] This applies to familial situations also. If we're faithfully centered in Christ, we're progressing in the grand plan, whether single or married, with or without children. We don't worship a marriage; we worship the Messiah.[15] Ultimately, in all this discussion of sealing, unless Christ will "seal [us] his" (Mosiah 5:15), we won't be sealed to any of ours.

2. ***Develop Christlike Attributes.*** As we come unto Christ, "grace for grace" (Doctrine and Covenants 93:20), the Lord will change and transform us to better enable us to abide in enduring relationships. We can all

work on receiving these holy attributes, becoming the very type of people we'd like to live with. Thus, sincere and continual repentance is essential. The Lord requires our hearts. Let's extend forgiveness and mercy and be patient with others' imperfections (as we'd like others to do for us[16]). Key is receiving the gift of charity—experiencing the love of God—which spiritual gift helps us to suffer long, be kind, act humbly, be selfless, control emotions, think righteously, and more (see Moroni 7:45). Let us pray with all the energy of our soul to be filled with this transforming love. Falling in love is not as crucial as developing divine disposition to *remain* in love. It is in abiding in our gospel covenant with Jesus that we develop the capacity to continue in a marriage covenant with our spouse. Developing Christlike attributes enables us to abide in trusted, safe, selfless, loving, dedicated, and empowered eternal families.

3. *Focus on Family.* All of us come from and have family connections. No person is an island. If heaven is relational and priesthood parental, then embrace those elements in your current sacred,[17] respective role(s): husband, wife, parent, grandparent, child, sibling, stepfamily, aunt, uncle, cousin, in-law, and the like. Value motherhood and fatherhood. Praise equal partnership in marriage. Place loving your family as central to your life. Nurture your proximate relationships where you

can. Sacrifice and give yourself for them. No other success can compensate for failure to do so.[18] Covenants are made in the sanctity of the temple but kept in the everyday laboratory of the home.[19] No matter how grand or modest, seek to establish a living space where the Spirit of the Lord can be present. Do your part (where you can) to cause to continue the laws, ordinances, and practices of the restored gospel: regular home study of scripture, prayer, singing or playing sacred music, observing the Sabbath day, service, home evening, and so on.[20] These family-centric practices are important to the *summum bonum* of priesthood.

4. ***Build Righteous Relationships.*** If the work of sealing is eternal ministering to serve, lift, build, teach, and reach others, we can all apply ourselves in that role immediately (elders quorum and Relief Society presidents, rejoice!). Visit that neighbor and express your love and faith. Listen to their concerns or needs and try to help where you can. Seek joy in lifting the weak, finding the lost, shepherding the wandering, inviting the prodigal. You're practicing a form of the great network! Learn how to work with and respect others equally in your labors in a spirit of interdependence, particularly between genders. Live righteous priesthood principles in everyday interactions: gentleness, meekness, kindness, temperance, love, etc. Be honest. No, seriously, be

honest. Respect others' agency. If God doesn't coerce, no unrighteous dominion should find place in our ways at work, home, or play. Learn to be temperate and circumscribe passions, developing meekness and an integrity of character that can be trusted by others, including God. Admittedly these are extremely tall orders, but so is the Sermon on the Mount. These are essential relational qualities to develop in our becoming more like God.

5. ***Be Endowed with Power.*** Each of us can become worthy and prepared to be endowed in the house of the Lord and receive its promissory blessings, which point to potential exalted marriage and family for all the faithful. Your endowment empowers you as a lawful heir in the covenant lineage of Abraham. Become a rightful heir by keeping the covenant commitments you made therein. Every kingdom has a law given, including the celestial. Learn to live the divine laws presented to you in the temple, as light cleaves to light. Learn to be governed by heavenly law and you will be preserved by heavenly law (see Doctrine and Covenants 88:34, 36, 40). Worship in the house of the Lord as often as your circumstances permit. Seek to become endowed with spiritual priesthood power (what other power could it be?[21]) over time by faithfully living the concepts and covenants presented in the temple endowment presentation. As you keep your

covenants, the Holy Spirit of Promise will ratify and seal upon you all promised blessings that have been bestowed upon your head.

6. *Seal All You Can.* As a son or daughter of Levi, participate in the great offering of the last days and latter-day Church to find and bind up the entire family of God through the covenants and ordinances of the holy priesthood. This happens one by one, so all our consecrated efforts and individual offerings are needed. Search through those ancestral records. Index that data. Take those names to the house of the Lord. Offer up, in similitude of the Savior, vicarious ordinances in their behalf, from baptism up through sealing. Do it for everyone you can and help create the great priesthood network of God. The Prophet Joseph Smith once said: "If you have power to seal on earth & in heaven then we should be crafty the first thing you do go & seal on earth your sons & daughters unto yourself & yourself unto your fathers in eternal glory & go ahead and not go back but use a little craftiness & seal all you can & when you get to heaven tell your father that what you seal on earth should be sealed in heaven."[22] Let's seal all we can.

7. *Wait on the Lord in Patience, Faith, and Hope.* God's promises come in His own way and time (see Doctrine and Covenants 88:68). Much of what Jesus

taught about restoration was *future* restoration. Future bodies. Future heaven. Future recompense. Future relationships. However, what we do today matters because now is the sowing season, and the seeds we must sow are faith, hope, and patience in God's promises. "Shew the same diligence to the full assurance of hope . . . Who through *faith and patience inherit the promises*" (Hebrews 6:11–12; emphasis added). Hope is to see afar off,[23] living now like future blessings are already obtained (see 1 Nephi 5:5). This hope is born through understanding and relying on the teachings, Atonement, and divine promises of Christ (see Moroni 7:41). Wait patiently upon the Lord when it comes to your family sealing promises. Don't give up on the dream. "The Lord knoweth all things from the beginning; wherefore, he prepareth a way to accomplish all his works among the children of men; for behold, he hath all power unto the fulfilling of all his words" (1 Nephi 9:6). Trust in His infinite goodness, mercy, and grace to work out challenging, unique, or inequitable situations. Rely on Him to heal and restore fallen aspects of your family. Don't let fear override your faith about celestial living conditions. He honors everyone's agency.[24] We know God is good and doesn't do anything unless it benefits the world, because He loves the world (see 2 Nephi 26:24). He loves you. He loves your family. Trust Him in patience. Look afar off. His promises are sure. "For since the beginning of the world have not men heard nor perceived by the ear, neither hath any eye seen, O God, besides thee, how great things thou hast prepared for him that waiteth for thee" (Doctrine and Covenants 133:45).

FUTURE RELATIONSHIPS

Although some eternal aspects of sealing are obscured in the twilight of mortality (for now), we hope this book has spread some divine rays of light on this central subject, increasing your vision and inspiring your soul. To summarize, an eternal sealing is:

- The dream, God's divine organization of heaven.
- The glory, priesthood's grand secret of power centered in eternal posterity.
- The hearts, uniting a man and woman together by covenant in eternal love to do God's work and become like Him.
- The heirs, creating a rightful and lawful royal priesthood lineage of covenant.
- The network, connecting the entire family of God to facilitate the blessings of eternity to everyone.
- The offering, performing ordinances for all

God's children in the temple so that none are lost.
- The Mediator, by whom all the family of God are organized and restored in their rightful condition.

In a real and coming day, this mortality will put on immortality. Mountains are laid low and valleys exalted. Heaven meets earth, to make earth our heaven. The dust that obeys God's voice flies like a storm unearthing caskets, ossuaries, and bones. At the sound of Michael's trump we see graves open. Elements meld. Bodies reform, breaking out from earth in transcendent light. The breath of life surges back through nostrils. Eyes see and the soul's window reflects again. Hands open and close, arms flex, and legs stand. Spirit courses through veins and bodies. No hairs of any head are lost. Everything and everyone is restored to their proper and perfect frame in incommensurate beauty, glory, and majesty. Souls are sanctified, sin and error removed. Clothed upon with righteousness, we are brought triumphant through the air to the pleasing bar of the great Jehovah. Risen, we now fall. New knees bow. Tongues of angels confess: "Blessed be the name of God! Hosannah to the highest!" We bathe His feet with our tears. We kiss Him and see His loving face.

THE HOLY SEALING

Arms reach for loved ones. Where are they? Will they be found? Yes. Sealing ties bind like divine tentacles, connecting lawful and rightful heirs preserved by priesthood and linked by love. We embrace. We choose one another. We claim. The Holy Spirit seals and ratifies. We organize by families. We love. We serve. We reach. We continue to learn and progress, grace by grace, together. We receive principalities, powers, and dominions. We inherit all that the Father has, even crowns of glory, immortality, and eternal lives. Kings and queens become gods, and we learn the ways of God. What are they? Priesthood and parenthood. We are family—the celestial pattern—sealed and secured through our mediating Savior, to whom we give glory forever and ever. Amen.

APPENDIX

PROMISES TO POSTERITY

The statements below form a representative list of promises from prophets to faithful, sealed parents regarding their posterity. Some of these statements were published in a September 2002 *Ensign* article, "Hope for Parents of Wayward Children."[1] It is not a comprehensive list, but we hope it is sufficiently broad to show repeated expression and emphasis over the years:

Joseph Smith:

"The covenants of the fathers with relation to the children and the covenants of the children in relation to the Fathers [is] that they may have the privilege of entering into the same in order to effect their mutual Salvation . . . Which when a [sealed] Father & Mother of a family have entered into[,] their children who have not transgressed[2] are secured by the seal wherewith the Parents have been sealed— And this is the Oath of God unto our Father Abraham and this doctrine shall stand forever."[3]

Brigham Young:

"Let the father and mother, who are members of this Church and kingdom, take a righteous course, and strive with all their might never to do a wrong, but to do good all their lives; if they have one child or one hundred children, if they conduct themselves towards them as they should, binding them to the Lord by their faith and prayers, I care not where those children go, they are bound up to their parents by an everlasting tie, and no power of earth or hell can separate them from their parents in eternity; they will return again to the fountain from whence they sprang."[4]

Lorenzo Snow:

"[Faithful parents] will, by the power of the Priesthood, work and labor, as the Son of God has, until you get all your sons and daughters in the path of exaltation and glory. This is just as sure as that the sun rose this morning over yonder mountains. Therefore, mourn not because all your sons and daughters do not follow in the path that you have marked out to them, or give heed to your counsels. Inasmuch as we succeed in securing eternal glory, and stand as saviors, and as kings and priests to our God, we will save our posterity."[5]

ORSON F. WHITNEY:

"The Prophet Joseph Smith declared . . . that the eternal sealings of faithful parents and the divine promises made to them for valiant service in the Cause of Truth, would save not only themselves, but likewise their posterity. Though some of the sheep may wander, the eye of the Shepherd is upon them, and sooner or later they will feel the tentacles of Divine Providence reaching out after them and drawing them back to the fold. Either in this life or the life to come, they will return. They will have to pay their debt to justice; they will suffer for their sins; and may tread a thorny path; but if it leads them at last, like the penitent Prodigal, to a loving and forgiving father's heart and home, the painful experience will not have been in vain. Pray for your careless and disobedient children; hold on to them with your faith. Hope on, trust on, till you see the salvation of God."[6]

APPENDIX

Joseph Fielding Smith:

He taught that children who are born in the covenant—and those who are sealed to their parents in the temple—"have claims upon the blessings of the gospel beyond what those not so born are entitled to receive. They may receive a greater guidance, a greater protection, a greater inspiration from the Spirit of the Lord; and then there is no power that can take them away from their parents."[7]

James E. Faust:

"Children of eternal sealings may have visited upon them the divine promises made to their valiant forebears who nobly kept their covenants. Covenants remembered by parents will be remembered by God. The children may thus become beneficiaries and inheritors of these great covenants and promises. This is because they are the children of the covenant."[8]

Boyd K. Packer:

"It is not uncommon for responsible parents to lose one of their children, for a time, to influences over which they have no control. . . . It is my conviction that those wicked influences one day will be overruled. . . . We cannot overemphasize the value of temple marriage, the binding ties of the sealing ordinance, and the standards of worthiness required of them. When parents keep the covenants they have made at the altar of the temple, their children will be forever bound to them."[9]

Henry B. Eyring:

"The story of the prodigal son gives us all hope. The prodigal remembered home, as will your children. They will feel your love drawing them back to you. Elder Orson F. Whitney, in a general conference of 1929, gave a remarkable promise, which I know is true, to the faithful parents who honor the temple sealing to their children."[10]

To be clear, as Elder David A. Bednar taught when reviewing similar parental sealing promises, we shouldn't misconstrue these powerful statements "to mean that wayward children unconditionally receive the blessings of salvation because of and through the faithfulness of parents. . . . Ultimately, a child must exercise his or her moral agency and respond in faith, repent with full purpose of heart, and act in accordance with the teachings of Christ."[11] In a sealing blessing, the Prophet Joseph Smith promised Sarah Ann Whitney

APPENDIX

that "all her Fathers house Shall be Saved in the Same Eternal glory and if any of them Shall wander from the foald of the Lord they Shall not perish but Shall return Saith the Lord and be Saived in and by repentance be crowned with all the fullness of the glory of the Everlasting gospel." Notice the phrase, "and by repentance."[12] As Orson F. Whitney indicated, rebellious children of the covenant will need to voluntarily choose to repent and realign their lives with God's will and suffer the consequences of their sins. None of this absolves any from heavenly justice.[13] But in this life or the next, the sealing promises and patriarchal priesthood can exert a "heavenly pull or tug that entices a wandering child to return to the fold eventually," as Elder Bednar described.[14]

NOTES

Epigraph

Discourse, 21 January 1844, as Reported by Wilford Woodruff, 182, The Joseph Smith Papers.

Authors' Note

1. There are books with chapters that explore sealing more academically, such as Jonathan Stapley's *The Power of Godliness: Mormon Liturgy and Cosmology* (Oxford University Press, 2018), Samuel Brown's *In Heaven as it is On Earth: Joseph Smith and the Early Mormon Conquest of Death* (Oxford University Press, 2012), or David Buerger's *The Mysteries of Godliness: A History of Mormon Temple Worship* (Signature Books, 2002). However, very few, if any, have attempted to explore and explain the broader work of sealing to everyday Latter-day Saints.
2. "Sealing Policies," *General Handbook*, 38.4–38.4.2.8, Gospel Library (as of Sept. 2024).
3. See Dallin H. Oaks, "Kingdoms of Glory," *Liahona*, November 2023.
4. Boyd K. Packer, "Little Children," *Ensign*, November 1986.
5. Elder Parley P. Pratt taught of sealing: "This last key of the priesthood is the most sacred of all, and pertains exclusively to the first presidency of the church, without whose sanction and approval or authority, no sealing blessing shall be administered" (Parley P. Pratt,

NOTES

in *Millennial Star*, Vol 5:149–53, March 1845). See also "Sealing," Church History Topics.

6. D. Todd Christofferson, "The Sealing Power," *Liahona*, November 2023.
7. Elder Dale G. Renlund taught, "Not being sealed to a spouse does not halt your progression in your discipleship to the Savior" ("Stronger and Closer Connection to God Through Multiple Covenants," BYU devotional, March 5, 2024).
8. Elder D. Todd Christofferson taught, "This sealing power is a perfect manifestation of the justice, mercy, and love of God" ("The Sealing Power," *Liahona*, November 2023).
9. President James E. Faust taught, "This sealing power thus reveals itself in family relationships, in attributes and virtues developed in a nurturing environment, and in loving service. These are the cords that bind families together, and the priesthood advances their development" ("Fathers, Mothers, Marriage," *Ensign*, August 2004).

Chapter 1: The Dream

1. Journal History of The Church of Jesus Christ of Latter-day Saints, 23 Feb. 1847, 362–64, Historical Department Archives, The Church of Jesus Christ of Latter-day Saints, CR 100 137, https://catalog.churchofjesuschrist.org/assets/75cc4e9f-bfcb-4ac2-8309-19d1a3e82e8e/0/361.
2. See R. Devan Jensen, Michael A. Goodman, and Barbara Morgan Gardner, "'Line upon Line': Joseph Smith's Growing Understanding of the Eternal Family," *Religious Educator* 20, no. 1 (2019). See also Carl Cranney, "'Led Just Right': The Theological Development of Vertical Latter-day Saint Sealings through 1894," *Mormon Historical Studies,* (2019), 77.
3. Joseph's journal for this day has a shorthand summary of this and simply reads, "Joseph— & J[ames] Adams "w-r m-r-r-d [were married]" which, based on the next day's marriages, Joseph Smith Papers historians interpret to mean "that JS and Adams were married for eternity to their respective wives Emma Smith and Harriet Denton Adams" (note 457). "Journal, December 1842–June 1844; Book 2, 10 March 1843–14 July 1843," [225], The Joseph Smith Papers.
4. See "Joseph Smith Discourse, 21 January 1844, as Reported by Wilford Woodruff," [182], The Joseph Smith Papers.
5. This would not begin until 1877 in Saint George, Utah. See Richard E. Bennett, "Wilford Woodruff and the Rise of Temple

NOTES

Consciousness among the Latter-day Saints, 1877–84," in *Banner of the Gospel: Wilford Woodruff*, ed. Alexander L. Baugh and Susan Easton Black (Religious Studies Center, Brigham Young University, and Deseret Book, 2010), 233–50.

6. This practice was known as the "law of adoption" and was practiced from the mid-1840s through the mid-1890s. See Richard E. Bennett, *Temples Rising* (2020), 126. Connecting into the covenant priesthood lineage of God through the nucleus of Latter-day prophets and apostles can also provide insight into some of the early practice and theology of plural marriage (see Brian Hales, *Joseph Smith's Polygamy, Volume 3: Theology* [Greg Kofford Books, 2013], 167; see also Richard Lyman Bushman, *Joseph Smith: Rough Stone Rolling* [Knopf, 2005], 440; Gospel Topics, "Plural Marriage in Kirtland and Nauvoo," Gospel Library).

7. Brigham Young felt that this practice of adoption to prophets was not ideal. "Had the keys of the priesthood been handed down from father to son throughout all generations . . . there would have been no necessity of the law of adoption, for we would all have been included in the covenant without it" (General Church Minutes, 12 March 1848, CR 100 3:18).

8. Apostle Heber C. Kimball told Wilford Woodruff: "He [Kimball] said that He did not Believe in this custom of Adoption that had been practiced in this Church. No man should give his Birthright to another but should keep his birthright in the linage of his Fathers & go to & unite the link through the whole linnage of their fathers until they come up to a man in the Linage who hild the priesthood. . . . Now unless a man is a poor Cuss he should keep his priesthood & unite with his Fathers & not give it to another" (Wilford Woodruff's Journal, 5:3–4, January 3, 1857).

9. Brigham said to Joseph in the dream, "The brethren have a great anxiety to understand the law of adoption or sealing principles" (Journal History of The Church of Jesus Christ of Latter-day Saints, 23 Feb. 1847, 362–64, Historical Department Archives, The Church of Jesus Christ of Latter-day Saints, CR 100 137 https://catalog.churchofjesus christ.org/assets/75cc4e9f-bfcb-4ac2-8309-19d1a3e82e8e/0/361).

10. Journal History of The Church of Jesus Christ of Latter-day Saints, 23 Feb. 1847, 362–64, Historical Department Archives, The Church of Jesus Christ of Latter-day Saints, CR 100 137, https://catalog.church

ofjesuschrist.org/assets/75cc4e9f-bfcb-4ac2-8309-19d1a3e82e8e/0/361.
11. "God Loveth His Children," Gospel Library, https://www.churchofjesuschrist.org/study/manual/god-loveth-his-children/god-loveth-his-children?lang=ase.
12. See Doctrine and Covenants 49:15. "The Family: A Proclamation to the World" teaches, "The family is central to the Creator's plan for the eternal destiny of His children."
13. See Joseph Smith's teaching to the recently formed Quorum of the Twelve Apostles prior to their endowment of power in Kirtland, Ohio (Discourse, 12 November 1835, 34, The Joseph Smith Papers).
14. See Revelation 7:2–4. Of these verses, Joseph Smith taught, "Four destroying angels holding power over the four quarters of the earth, until the servants of God are sealed in their foreheads which signifies sealing the blessing upon their heads meaning the everlasting covenant, thereby making their calling and election sure." His further comments were written but crossed out, "What is the full extend of that seal? Shall I tell you? No. Doctrine <of> Election— Sealing of the servants of our God on the top of their heads— 'tis not the cross, as the Catholics would have it" (History, 1838–1856, volume E-1 [1 July 1843–30 April 1844], 1690, The Joseph Smith Papers).
15. See various synonyms for "seal" at https://www.thesaurus.com/browse/seal or "Sealing," Church History Topics, https://www.churchofjesuschrist.org/study/history/topics/sealing?lang=eng.
16 Journal History of The Church of Jesus Christ of Latter-day Saints, 23 Feb. 1847, 362–64, Historical Department Archives, The Church of Jesus Christ of Latter-day Saints, CR 100 137, https://catalog.churchofjesuschrist.org/assets/75cc4e9f-bfcb-4ac2-8309-19d1a3e82e8e/0/361.
17. Bruce Hafen, *Covenant Hearts* (Deseret Book, 2005), 60.
18. Such examples include mothers sealed to first husbands who aren't sealed to their second but have children with the second spouse, leading to questions on whom the child is sealed to.
19. Such as sealing deceased women to all their known husbands, sealing parents or grandparents who knowingly weren't happy together or decidedly against the Church, or not being able to seal due to unknown family history lines.
20. See *General Handbook*, section 38.4 as of September 2024.

NOTES

21. See Jenet Erickson, "Designed for Covenant Relationships," BYU devotional, November 8, 2022.
22. Elder Jeffrey R. Holland taught, "I don't know how to speak about heaven in the traditional, lovely, paradisiacal beauty that we speak of heaven; I wouldn't know how to speak of heaven, without my wife or my children. It would not be heaven for me" (as cited in "Scott Taylor: For Elder Holland, heaven without his wife and children 'wouldn't be heaven for me'" *Church News*, July 22, 2023).
23. Thank you and credit to Janiece Johnson for this insight and phrase.
24. John Taylor discourse, October 7, 1859, *Journal of Discourses* 7:318.
25. Joseph Smith once famously said of heavenly teachings, "This is good doctrine; it tastes good" (History, 1838–1856, volume E-1 [1 July 1843–30 April 1844], 1974, The Joseph Smith Papers.
26. "The Family: A Proclamation to the World."
27. Dallin H. Oaks, "Trust in the Lord," *Liahona*, November 2019.
28. See "The Family: A Proclamation to the World": "The divine plan of happiness enables family relationships to be perpetuated beyond the grave."

Chapter 2: The Glory

1. See Andrew H. Hedges, "'They Pursue Me without Cause': Joseph Smith in Hiding and D&C 127, 128," *Religious Educator* 16, no. 1 (2015): 43–59.
2. See "Historical Introduction," Letter to the Church, 7 September 1842 [Doctrine and Covenants 128], 1, The Joseph Smith Papers.
3. See "summum bonum" in Oxford Language dictionary, or Merriam-Webster https://www.merriam-webster.com/dictionary/summum%20bonum.
4. See Russell M. Nelson, "Ministering with the Power and Authority of God," *Ensign*, May 2018.
5. See Dallin H. Oaks, "Keys and Authority of the Priesthood," *Ensign*, May 2014; Russell M. Nelson, "Spiritual Treasures," *Ensign*, November 2019; Conversation with General Relief Society Presidency Jean Bingham, Sharon Eubank, and Reyna Aburto in *Church News*, "Why Women in the Church Should Follow President Nelson's Invitation to Study about the Priesthood," March 6, 2020; J. Anette Dennis, "Accessing God's Power Through Covenants," 2024 Worldwide Relief Society Devotional.
6. "Priesthood Principles," *General Handbook*, 3.0, 3.5 as of September 2024.

NOTES

7. This order of priesthood is temple-centric. Doctrine and Covenants 131 describes eternal marriage as an "order of the priesthood" (v. 2). When instructing the Nauvoo Female Relief Society (which originally was a select society also helping women prepare for the temple, like a school of the prophets), Elder Reynolds Cahoon said, "the Order of th[e] Priesthood is not complete without [the women of Relief Society]" and Mary Isabella Horn wrote, "the Priesthood was not firmly established on the earth, without an organization of this kind" ("Mary Isabella Horne and Others, Letter to Salt Lake Stake Relief Society, January 15, 1878," as cited in *The First Fifty Years of Relief Society* [Church Historian's Press, 2016], 425).
8. "A group of people united in a formal way" ("order" as a noun in Merriam-Webster Dictionary, https://www.merriam-webster.com/dictionary/order).
9. See "the name Melchizedek" at https://www.abarim-publications.com/Meaning/Melchizedek.html. *Melchizedek* can also mean "my king is righteous" (see https://www.britannica.com/biography/Melchizedek).
10. Boyd K. Packer taught, "Of all the other titles that He could have used, He chose to be called 'Father.' . . . His use of the name 'Father' is a lesson for all as we come to understand what it is that matters most in this life" ("The Witness," *Ensign*, May 2014).
11. David O. McKay taught, "Parenthood is next to Godhood" (*Teachings of Presidents of the Church: David O. McKay* [2011], xxvii).
12. In 1909, the First Presidency of the Church taught, "All men and women are in the similitude of the universal Father and Mother, and are literally the sons and daughters of Deity" ("The Origin of Man," *Improvement Era* 13, no. 1 [Nov. 1909]: 78). See also Gospel Topics, "Mother in Heaven," Gospel Library.
13. Discourse, 7 April 1844, as Published in Times and Seasons, 614, The Joseph Smith Papers.
14. See Gospel Topics, "Becoming Like God," Gospel Library.
15. See Julie B. Beck, "Teaching the Doctrine of the Family," Address to CES Religious Educators, 2009, 3.
16. Eliza R. Snow taught, "You, my sisters, if you are faithful will become Queens of Queens, and Priestesses unto the Most High God. These are your callings" (as cited in *The First Fifty Years of Relief Society* [Church Historian's Press, 2016], 388). See also Anthony Sweat,

NOTES

The Holy Invitation (Deseret Book, 2017) and *The Holy Covenants* (Deseret Book, 2022).

17. Joseph Smith taught: "You need an endowment . . . in order that you may be prepared and able to overcome all things" (Discourse, 12 November 1835, 34, The Joseph Smith Papers). See also Anthony Sweat, "We Need an Endowment," BYU devotional, April 5, 2022.
18. President Dallin H. Oaks said, "The culminating ordinance in the restored Church is the everlasting covenant of marriage, which makes possible the perpetuation of glorious family relationships" ("The Need for a Church," *Liahona*, November 2021).
19. Russell M. Nelson has taught, "No man in this Church can obtain the highest degree of celestial glory without a worthy woman who is sealed to him. This temple ordinance enables eventual exaltation for both of them" ("Salvation and Exaltation," *Ensign*, May 2008).
20. See M. Russell Ballard, "This Is My Work and Glory," *Ensign*, May 2013.
21. "The government in the family follows the patriarchal pattern, differing in some respects from priesthood leadership in the Church" (Ulisses Soares, "In Partnership with the Lord," *Liahona*, November 2022).
22. See Ulisses Soares, "In Partnership with the Lord," *Liahona*, November 2022.
23. Russell M. Nelson explained that with Adam, "Eve served in matriarchal partnership with the patriarchal priesthood" ("Lessons from Eve," *Ensign*, November 1987).
24. For a summary, see "Equal Partnership in Marriage," Lesson 17, *The Eternal Family Teacher Material Religion 200*, 2022.
25. "What I Hope You Will Teach Your Children about the Temple," *Ensign*, August 1985.
26. "History, 1838–1856, volume D-1 [1 August 1842–1 July 1843]," 1551, The Joseph Smith Papers.
27. Dallin H. Oaks, "Two Great Commandments," *Ensign*, November 2019.
28. This promise has been given many times in many places. See, among many other examples, *General Handbook*, 2.1; Dallin H. Oaks, "The Great Plan of Happiness," *Ensign*, November 1993; Howard W. Hunter, "The Church Is for All People," *Ensign*, June 1989.
29. Discourse, 7 April 1844, as Published in Times and Seasons, 614, The Joseph Smith Papers.

NOTES

30. See Bruce Hafen, *Covenant Hearts: Why Marriage Matters, and How to Make it Last* (Deseret Book, 2012).

Chapter 3: The Hearts

1. See *Benjamin F. Johnson, My Life's Review* (Zion's Printing and Publishing Co., 1947), 81.
2. Johnson, *My Life's Review*, 82.
3. Johnson, *My Life's Review*, 89.
4. Johnson, *My Life's Review*, 89.
5. Johnson, *My Life's Review*, 93.
6. History Draft [1 March–31 December 1843], 31, The Joseph Smith Papers.
7. History Draft [1 March–31 December 1843], 31, The Joseph Smith Papers.
8. Johnson, *My Life's Review*, 25.
9. Johnson, *My Life's Review*, 126. It should be acknowledged here that Joseph Smith was also teaching Benjamin Johnson about plural marriage at this time, and this quote derives from some of those teachings. Early Church doctrines of eternal marriage and plural marriage were not discrete, but instead grew out as branches from the same sealing doctrine and "were inextricably combined into one unfolding story in Nauvoo," according to historian Brian Hales (*Joseph Smith's Polygamy: Vol. 1*, [Greg Kofford Books, 2013], 223).
10. While Benjamin's recollection doesn't say specifically that they took one another's hand, to do so is consistent with other weddings Joseph performed. See his marriage of Newel and Lydia Goldthwaite Bailey on November 24, 1835. Journal, 1835–1836, 49, The Joseph Smith Papers.
11. William Clayton, Journal, 16 May and 19–20 Oct. 1843. See also Journal, December 1842–June 1844; Book 3, 15 July 1843–29 February 1844, 139, The Joseph Smith Papers.
12. Johnson, *My Life's Review*, 93.
13. At the funeral of Patricia T. Holland, wife of President Jeffrey R. Holland, President Russell M. Nelson taught that the most important day of her life was not her birthday or day of her death: "Her most important date was June 7, 1963, when she and Jeff were sealed in the St. George Temple. This ordinance sealed them together forever" (as cited in Sarah Jane Weaver, "'What a celestial woman looks like': Sister Patricia T. Holland is remembered for her faith, testimony, loving heart and example," *Church News*, July 28, 2023).

NOTES

14. Steven Covey wrote insightfully: "Interdependent people combine their own efforts with the efforts of others to achieve their greatest success" (*Seven Habits of Highly Successful People* [Simon & Schuster UK, 2020]), Reissue edition, May 19, 2020).
15. President Dallin H. Oaks taught: "Our theology begins with heavenly parents. Our highest aspiration is to be like them" (Dallin H. Oaks, "Apostasy and Restoration," *Ensign,* May 1995).
16. Russell M. Nelson, "The Temple and Your Spiritual Foundation," *Liahona*, November 2021.
17. See "Eternal Life," Gospel Topics and Questions, https://www.churchofjesuschrist.org/study/manual/gospel-topics/eternal-life?lang=eng; see also Camille Fronk Olson, "To Know God Is Life Eternal," in *Let Us Reason Together: Essays in Honor of the Life's Work of Robert L. Millet*, ed. J. Spencer Fluhman and Brent L. Top (Religious Studies Center, 2016), 23–36.
18. Russell M. Nelson, "Celestial Marriage," *Ensign*, November 2008.
19. Dale G. Renlund, "Stronger and Closer Connection to God Through Multiple Covenants," BYU devotional, March 5, 2024.
20. "Cleave," https://www.merriam-webster.com/dictionary/cleave. *Cleave* can also mean to divide or split apart. In this context the command and word is used to come together.
21. President Spencer W. Kimball gave this dual rendering in Conference Report, October 1962, 56–58.
22. See "Section 42, The Law of the Lord," *Doctrine and Covenants Student Manual* (2002), 82–86.
23. "Husband and Wife," *General Handbook*, 2.1.2 as of September 2024.
24. "Husband and Wife," *General Handbook*, 2.1.2 as of September 2024.
25. Matthew L. Carpenter, "Fruit That Remains," *Liahona*, May 2024.
26. See David A. Bednar, "Things as They Really Are 2.0," Worldwide Devotional for Young Adults, November 3, 2024.
27. See Jeffrey R. Holland, "Of Souls, Symbols, and Sacraments," BYU devotional, January 12, 1988.
28. See Dale G. Renlund and Ruth Lybbert Renlund, "The Divine Purposes of Sexual Intimacy," *Ensign*, August 2020.
29. "The Family: A Proclamation to the World," Gospel Library.
30. "Being united in marriage requires a full partnership, sharing responsibilities. A husband and wife are equal in God's eyes. One should not dominate the other ("Husband and Wife," *General Handbook* 2.1.2 as of September 2024).

NOTES

31. "Adam and Eve set an example for husbands and wives . . . they were united with each other and with God" (*General Handbook* 2.1.2, as of September 2024).
32. Quentin L. Cook taught, "When a man and woman are sealed in the temple . . . they obtain and receive priesthood blessings and power to direct the affairs of their family. . . . They have equal power to receive revelation for their family. When they work together in love and righteousness, their decisions are heaven blessed" ("Great Love for Our Father's Children," *Ensign*, May 2019).
33. The Family Proclamation teaches, "Fathers and mothers are . . . equal partners." President Nelson said, "If you are married, counsel with your wife as your equal partner" (Russell M. Nelson, "What We Are Learning and Will Never Forget," *Liahona*, May 2021).
34. L. Tom Perry taught, "There is not a president or a vice president in a family. The couple works together eternally for the good of the family. They are united together in word, in deed, and in action as they lead, guide, and direct their family unit. They are on equal footing. They plan and organize the affairs of the family jointly and unanimously as they move forward" (L. Tom Perry, "Fatherhood, an Eternal Calling," *Ensign*, May 2004). See also Ulisses Soares, "In Partnership with the Lord," which teaches, husbands and wives should "not position themselves as president or vice president of their family" (*Liahona*, November 2022).
35. See Dallin H. Oaks, "Priesthood Authority in the Family and the Church," *Ensign*, November 2005; Boyd K. Packer, "The Relief Society," *Ensign*, May 1998. See also Barbara Morgan Gardner, "Connecting Daughters of God with His Priesthood Power," *Liahona*, March 2019; see also her chapter "The Temple and the Patriarchal Order of the Priesthood," in her book *The Priesthood Power of Women: In The Temple, Church, and Family* (Deseret Book, 2019).
36. See Ulisses Soares, "In Partnership with the Lord." "A husband and wife are equal in God's eyes. One should not dominate the other. Their decisions should be made in unity and love, with full participation of both" (*General Handbook* 2.1.2 as of September 2024).
37. This is a summary of many principles taught about divine counseling by the Lord's servants in various places, such as in "Learning from God's Pattern of Councils," *Liahona*, June 12, 2022; M. Russell Ballard, "Family Councils," *Liahona*, May 2016; "Counseling with Councils Is Lord's System, Elder Ballard Declares," *Church News*,

NOTES

January 11, 2017; "Councils Follow Heavenly Pattern, Say Leaders in Roundtable Discussion," *Church News*, January 3, 2017; M. Russell Ballard, "Counseling with Our Councils," *Ensign*, May 1994.

38. See Dallin H. Oaks, "Following Christ," *Liahona*, November 2024.
39. Dallin H. Oaks, "The Melchizedek Priesthood and the Keys," *Ensign*, May 2020.
40. As President Oaks taught, all authority is priesthood. "What other authority can it be?" At another time he taught, "Priesthood authority is also exercised and its blessings realized in the families of Latter-day Saints. By families I mean a priesthood-holding man and a woman who are married and their children. I also include the variations from the ideal relationships such as caused by death or divorce" ("The Melchizedek Priesthood and the Keys," *Ensign*, May 2020). See also "From the Prophet Joseph Smith's day to ours, the ongoing restoration of all things has brought enlightenment on the necessity of the authority and power of the priesthood in helping both men and women accomplish their divinely appointed responsibilities" (Jean Bingham, "United in Accomplishing God's Work," *Ensign*, May 2020).
41. Russell M. Nelson, "Spiritual Treasures," *Ensign*, November 2019.
42. Russell M. Nelson, "The Temple and Your Spiritual Foundation," *Liahona*, November 2021.
43. President Dallin H. Oaks reiterated: "[God] will force no one into a sealing relationship against his or her will. The blessings of a sealed relationship are assured for all who keep their covenants but never by forcing a sealed relationship on another person who is unworthy or unwilling" ("Kingdoms of Glory," *Liahona*, November 2023).
44. Elder Dale G. Renlund taught, "Agency continues to be an overriding component of eternal marriage. No one will be forced to live in a marriage they do not choose or accept, even after the temple sealing" ("Stronger and Closer Connection to God Through Multiple Covenants," BYU Devotional, March 5, 2024).
45. Jean Bingham, "United in Accomplishing God's Work," *Ensign*, May 2020.
46. "The blessings of an eternal family are realized," the Church leaders write, "as members keep those covenants and repent when they fall short" (*General Handbook* 2.1.1 as of September 2024).
47. See Dale G. Renlund, "Stronger and Closer Connection to God Through Multiple Covenants," BYU devotional, March 5, 2024.

NOTES

48. See Neil L. Andersen, "Facing Mortality as Adults: Marriage, Children, and the Temple," BYU Idaho devotional, May 19, 2024.
49. William Clayton, Journal, 16 May and 19–20 Oct. 1843. See also Journal, December 1842–June 1844; Book 3, 15 July 1843–29 February 1844, 139, The Joseph Smith Papers. See also Steven C. Harper, "Section 131" in *Doctrine and Covenants Contexts* (Book of Mormon Central, 2021), 348–49.
50. See "Holy Spirit of Promise" in *Guide to the Scriptures*. Elder David A. Bednar said, "The Holy Spirit of Promise is the ratifying power of the Holy Ghost. When sealed by the Holy Spirit of Promise, an ordinance, vow, or covenant is binding on earth and in heaven (see Doctrine and Covenants 132:7). Receiving this 'stamp of approval' from the Holy Ghost is the result of faithfulness, integrity, and steadfastness in honoring gospel covenants 'in [the] process of time' (Moses 7:21). However, this sealing can be forfeited through unrighteousness and transgression" (Ye Must Be Born Again," *Ensign*, May 2007).
51. See Richard G. Scott, "Temple Worship: the Source of Strength in Times of Need," *Ensign*, May 2009; see also Cree-L Kofford, "Marriage in the Lord's Way: Part 1," *Ensign*, June 1998, and Matthew L. Carpenter, "Fruit That Remains," *Liahona*, May 2024.
52. Elder David A. Bednar taught at a BYU–Idaho devotional, "The house of the Lord—the sealing that takes place—is an opportunity. It is not a guarantee. It is predicated upon our faithfulness" ("In honor of their 50th wedding anniversary, Elder and Sister Bednar share lessons learned from marriage," *Church News*, March 11, 2025).
53. "Only those who are married in the temple and whose marriage is sealed by the Holy Spirit of Promise will continue as spouses after death" (Russell M. Nelson, "Celestial Marriage," *Ensign*, November 2008).

Chapter 4: The Heirs

1. In the summer/fall of 1832, more than 100 members from Ohio came to Zion without the "certificate" from the bishop required by revelation (see Doctrine and Covenants 72:16–18). Joseph Smith criticized this group saying they "they left here [Ohio] under this displeasure of heaven" and make "a mock of the profession of faith in the commandments by proceding contrary thereto [to Zion]" without "obtaining recommends" (Letter to William W. Phelps, 31 July 1832, 2, The Joseph Smith Papers).
2. An "inheritance" in the early Church "generally referred to land

NOTES

promised by or received from God for the church and its members," particularly in Independence, Missouri. See Doctrine and Covenants 38:19–20 ("Inheritance" https://www.josephsmithpapers.org/topic/inheritance).

3. This letter from Phelps is not known to exist, but in Joseph Smith's July 31 reply he says, "I have received your letter dated 30th June and procede this morning to answer it." The prophet addresses many questions in this letter, including criticisms of those who settled to Missouri without permission (Letter to William W. Phelps, 31 July 1832, 1, The Joseph Smith Papers).

4. As cited in Doctrine and Covenants 85:3–5, 11–12; See original in Letter to William W. Phelps, 27 November 1832, 2, The Joseph Smith Papers.

5. Nauvoo Relief Society Minute Book, 22, The Joseph Smith Papers.

6. Joseph Smith Journal, Apr. 28, 1842, in *The Joseph Smith Papers, Journals, Volume 2,* 52.

7. Bathsheba Smith recalled that Joseph Smith "wanted to make us, as the women were in Paul's day, 'A kingdom of priestesses.'. . . We have that ceremony in our endowments as Joseph taught" (as cited in *The First Fifty Years of Relief Society* [Church Historian's Press, 2016] "Introduction," xxviii).

8. See https://www.churchofjesuschrist.org/temples/sacred-temple-clothing?lang=eng.

9. See Russell M. Nelson, "The Everlasting Covenant," *Liahona*, October 2022. Joseph Smith once spoke on August 13, 1843, of "the doctrine of election and the sealing powers and principles; and spoke of the doctrine of election with the seed of Abraham and the sealing of blessings upon his posterity" (History, 1838–1856, volume E-1 [1 July 1843–30 April 1844], 1690, The Joseph Smith Papers).

10. Russell M. Nelson, "Children of the Covenant," *Ensign*, May 1995.

11. Joseph Smith once taught: "And though we cannot claim these promises which were made to the ancients, or that they are not our property merely because they were made to them, yet if we are the children of the most High, and are called with the same calling with which they were called, and embrace the same covenant that they embraced, and are faithful to the testimony of our Lord as they were, we can approach the Father in the name of Christ as they approached him, and for ourselves obtain the same promises" (Letter to the Church, circa March 1834, 144, The Joseph Smith Papers).

NOTES

12. See Dale G. Renlund, "Accessing God's Power," Relief Society devotional address, March 16, 2025.
13. See *General Handbook*, 38.4.2.8 as of September 2024. See also "If my parents were sealed in the temple and then got divorced, which one am I sealed to?" (*New Era*, August 2015).
14. See Russell M. Nelson, "The Everlasting Covenant," *Liahona*, October 2022.
15. "Our children who are born in the priesthood are legal heirs, and entitled to the revelations of the Lord, and as the Lord lives, his angels have charge over them" (*Discourses of Brigham Young*, 196); President Joseph Fielding Smith (1876–1972) taught that children who are born in the covenant—and those who are sealed to their parents in the temple—"have claims upon the blessings of the gospel beyond what those not so born are entitled to receive. They may receive a greater guidance, a greater protection, a greater inspiration from the Spirit of the Lord; and then there is no power that can take them away from their parents" (*Doctrines of Salvation*, comp. Bruce R. McConkie [1955], 2:90).
16. See Russell M. Nelson, "Let God Prevail," *Ensign*, November 2020.

Chapter 5: The Network

1. Joshua Matson, "Decoding the Self-Tracking Symbols of Wilford Woodruff's Journals," *BYU Studies Quarterly* 63, no. 1, 2024, 169. Special thanks to Dr. Matson for showing us this page of Wilford Woodruff's journal with the linked hearts.
2. See Joshua Matson, "Decoding the Self-Tracking Symbols of Wilford Woodruff's Journals," *BYU Studies Quarterly* 63, no. 1, 2024, 169, 176–78.
3. "Journal (January 1, 1843–December 31, 1844)," January 28, 1844, The Wilford Woodruff Papers.
4. "Journal (January 1, 1843–December 31, 1844)," January 28, 1844–January 31, 1844, The Wilford Woodruff Papers.
5. Joshua Matson writes of this drawing, "This symbol suggests that the sealing they [Wilford and Phebe] had received was not only joining them to one another but also connecting them to the fathers (Abraham, Isaac, Jacob, and so forth) and to other individuals who had received this ordinance, including many members of the Twelve and their wives" (Matson, 195–96).
6. Anthony has asked this question to thousands of students, and informally this is the typical answer.

NOTES

7. See former General Relief Society President, Julie B. Beck, "Teaching the Doctrine of the Family," Address to CES Religious Educators, 2009, 3. Referencing these same verses, President Russell M. Nelson taught, "If families were not sealed in holy temples, the whole earth would be utterly wasted" (Russell M. Nelson, "The Atonement," *Ensign*, November 1996).
8. Elder D. Todd Christofferson taught, "The power to validate all priesthood ordinances and make them binding both on earth and in heaven—the sealing power—is crucial for gathering and preparing a covenant people on both sides of the veil. . . . We tend to think of the sealing authority as applying only to certain temple ordinances, but that authority is necessary to make any ordinance valid and binding beyond death" ("The Sealing Power," *Liahona*, November 2023).
9. "Instruction on Priesthood, circa 5 October 1840," 9, The Joseph Smith Papers.
10. "Discourse, 10 March 1844, as Reported by Wilford Woodruff," [207], The Joseph Smith Papers. See also the link between Elijah's sealing keys and baptisms for the dead in Doctrine and Covenants 128:8–9.
11. See D. Todd Christofferson, "The Sealing Power," *Liahona*, November 2023.
12. Discourse, 21 January 1844, as Reported by Wilford Woodruff, 182, The Joseph Smith Papers.
13. See D. Todd Christofferson, "The Sealing Power," *Liahona*, November 2023.
14. This sacred circle of prayer has been mentioned publicly by the Church (see "Temple Prayer Roll Submission") and by Church leaders (see N. Eldon Tanner, "The Administration of the Church," *Ensign*, November 1979). See also "Prayer Circles," *Encyclopedia of Mormonism: The History, Scripture, Doctrine, and Procedure of The Church of Jesus Christ of Latter-day Saints* (Macmillan, 1992), 1120.
15. President Joseph F. Smith taught, "When messengers are sent to minister to the inhabitants of this earth, they are not strangers, but from the ranks of our kindred, friends, and fellow-beings and fellow servants. . . . In like manner, our fathers and mothers, brothers, sisters and friends who have passed away from this earth, having been faithful, and worthy to enjoy these rights and privileges, may have a mission given to them to visit their relatives and friends upon the earth again, bringing from the divine Presence messages of love, of warning, or reproof and instruction, to those whom they had learned

NOTES

to love in the flesh." (*Gospel Doctrine: Sermons and Writings of Joseph F. Smith*, [Deseret Book, 1986], 435–36). President James E. Faust taught: "Perhaps in this life we are not given to fully understand how enduring the sealing cords of righteous parents are to their children. It may very well be that there are more helpful sources at work than we know. I believe there is a strong familial pull as the influence of beloved ancestors continues with us from the other side of the veil" ("Dear Are the Sheep That Have Wandered," *Ensign*, May 2003). See also Jeffrey R. Holland, "The Ministry of Angels," *Ensign*, November 2008.

16. *Times and Seasons*, 2 May 1842, 776, The Joseph Smith Papers.
17. See "What's on the Other Side? A Conversation with Brent L. Top on the Spirit World," *Religious Educator* 14, no. 2 (2013), 48. See also Brent L. Top, *What's on the Other Side?* (Deseret Book, 2012).
18. "God Loveth His Children," *The Church of Jesus Christ of Latter-day Saints* (2007).
19. Elder L. Tom Perry said, "The entire theology of our restored gospel centers on families and on the new and everlasting covenant of marriage. . . . We also believe that strong traditional families are . . . the basic units of eternity and of the kingdom and government of God. We believe that the organization and government of heaven will be built around families and extended families" ("Why Marriage and Family Matter—Everywhere in the World," *Ensign*, May 2015).
20. President Ezra Taft Benson taught, "The Church was created in large measure to help the family, and long after the Church has performed its mission, the celestial patriarchal order will still be functioning" (*Teachings of Ezra Taft Benson,* 491).
21. *Teachings of Lorenzo Snow*, 138, as cited in *Eternal Marriage Student Manual* (2003), 138. See also *Teachings of the Presidents of the Church: Lorenzo Snow* (2012), 140.
22. "Journal, December 1842–June 1844; Book 3, 15 July 1843–29 February 1844," [73], The Joseph Smith Papers; spelling standardized by the authors for readability.

Chapter 6: The Offering

1. Orson Hyde, *The Latter-day Saints' Millennial Star* (Liverpool, England) 9, no. 2, 1847, 25.
2. Orson Hyde, *The Latter-day Saints' Millennial Star* (Liverpool, England) 9, no. 2, 1847, 23.

NOTES

3. Russell M. Nelson, "The Everlasting Covenant," *Liahona*, October 2022.
4. See Leviticus. See also American Bible Society "Temple Offerings," https://bibleresources.americanbible.org/resource/temple-offerings.
5. See Dale G. Renlund, "Family History and Temple Work: Sealing and Healing," *Ensign*, May 2018.
6. Discourse, 21 January 1844, as Reported by Wilford Woodruff, 182, The Joseph Smith Papers.
7. President Russell M. Nelson called this gathering of Israel on both sides of the veil "the greatest challenge, the greatest cause, the greatest work" ("The Everlasting Covenant," *Liahona*, October 2022).
8. "God wants to connect all people to the covenant He made anciently with Abraham" (Russell M. Nelson, "The Everlasting Covenant," *Liahona*, October 2022).
9. Elder Jeffrey R. Holland summarized that the allegory of the olive tree in Jacob 5 shows God's parental love for His children (*Christ and the New Covenant: The Messianic Message of the Book of Mormon* [Deseret Book, 1997], 165–66).
10. Russell M. Nelson, "Children of the covenant will be blessed—here and hereafter" ("Children of the Covenant," *Ensign*, May 1995).
11. See Daniel H. Ludlow, ed., *Encyclopedia of Mormonism*, 5 vols. [Macmillan, 1992], 3:1067, 1135.
12. See Dr. Eva Whitesman's insightful discussion on this concept on the *Follow Him* Podcast, Episode 26 on Alma 13–16, 2024, around time stamp 08:12.
13. See D. Todd Christofferson, "The Sealing Power," *Liahona*, November 2023.
14. See Bradley R. Wilcox, "O Youth of the Noble Birthright," *Liahona*, November 2024.
15. It is estimated there has been around 117 billion people that have lived on our planet. The *current* living population of 8 billion makes up almost 7 percent of all people who have ever lived. It took until 1800 for the world population to reach 1 billion, and took a sharp upward compounding increase ever since. In fact, "it took nearly seven centuries for the population to double from 0.25 billion (in the early 9th century) to 0.5 billion in the middle of the 16th century" but "things sped up considerably in the middle of the 20th century.

The fastest doubling of the world population happened between 1950 and 1987: a doubling from 2.5 to 5 billion people in *just 37*

NOTES

years — the population doubled within a little more than one generation" (Our World in Data, "World Population Growth" revised 2019, https://ourworldindata.org/world-population-growth). See also PRB "How Many People Have Ever Lived on Earth?" https://www.prb.org/articles/how-many-people-have-ever-lived-on-earth/ or "How Many People Have Ever Lived on Earth?" https://info.nicic.gov/ces/global/population-demographics/how-many-people-have-ever-lived-earth.

16. See David A. Bednar, "The Hearts of the Children Shall Turn," *Ensign*, November 2011. See also David A. Bednar, "To Sweep the Earth as with a Flood," (BYU Education Week address, August 2014). See also https://www.familysearch.org/en/blog/ai-developments-genealogy.
17. As an example, in 1955 there were nine total temples worldwide. As of writing this book, there are 350. That number has nearly doubled in the six years of Russell M. Nelson's presidency alone.
18. See Russell M. Nelson and Wendy W. Nelson, "Hope of Israel," Worldwide Youth Devotional, June 3, 2018.

Chapter 7: The Mediator

1. There's debate on the precise year of Jesus's death. But scholar Jeffrey R. Chadwick summarizes, "A broad majority of scholars maintain that AD 30 was the year in which Jesus was crucified at the season of Passover" (Dating the Death of Jesus Christ, *BYU Studies Quarterly* 54, no. 4, 2015, 139. For the hour of death, see Matthew 27:46, which places it "about the ninth hour." The Jewish day started at 6:00 a.m., which places the ninth hour at 3:00 p.m.
2. President Russell M. Nelson taught, "The fulfillment of the Abrahamic covenant becomes feasible because of the Atonement of our Savior, the Lord Jesus Christ. Jesus Christ is at the center of the Abrahamic covenant" ("The Everlasting Covenant," *Liahona*, October 2022).
3. Russell M. Nelson, "The Temple and Your Spiritual Foundation," *Liahona*, November 2021.
4. Elder Brian K. Taylor of the Seventy taught of the "significance and symbolic nature of the holy altar and its central position in the [sealing] room. . . . In this we see our Savior's atoning sacrifice. . . . We learn in this celestial setting it is only through and because of the Atonement and Resurrection of Jesus Christ that eternal families can be formed" ("The Sealing Covenant," Utah Area Broadcast, November 20, 2024). John Hilton writes that "the Crucifixion of Jesus

NOTES

Christ is literally at the center of the sealing ordinance" (*Considering the Cross* [Deseret Book, 2021], 199).

5. See "Wearing the Temple Garment," *General Handbook* 26.3.3.2 as of September 2024; See also, "Emphasizing Covenants, First Presidency updates temple recommend interview questions, shares statement on the wearing of the temple garment," *Church News*, April 14, 2024. Also "Garments," Topics and Questions, https://www.churchofjesus christ.org/study/manual/gospel-topics/garments?lang=eng.
6. *True to the Faith* says, "The word *atone* means to reconcile, or to restore to harmony" ("Atonement").
7. Boyd K. Packer, "The Brilliant Morning of Forgiveness," *Ensign,* November 1995.
8. Elder David A. Bednar taught, "Some of you have experienced great sorrow in abusive or dysfunctional family relationships. . . . Whatever bad things may have occurred in your family, I testify and promise that the Lord Jesus Christ is the source of the healing, renewing, and restoring that you need" ("A Welding Link," Worldwide Devotional for Young Adults, September 10, 2017).
9. Gerrit W. Gong, "Happy and Forever," *Liahona*, November 2022.
10. Credit to Dr. Adam Miller for his insight on this topic on the *Follow Him* podcast, Book of Mormon Episode 32, Alma 39–42, Part 1, roughly minutes 10:30–12:30.
11. See Anthony Sweat, "The Restoring Power of Christ," in *Christ In Every Hour* (Deseret Book, 2016).
12. Joseph Smith Papers, History, 1838–1856, volume D-1 [1 August 1842–1 July 1843], Page 1535.
13. *General Handbook,* 2.1 as of September 2024.
14. See Russell M. Nelson, "Joy and Spiritual Survival," *Liahona*, November 2016.
15. We thank and credit our BYU religious education colleague Dr. Ty Mansfield for this conceptual insight that we've phrased in our own words.
16. See Ulisses Soares, "In Partnership with the Lord," *Liahona*, November 2022.
17. "All family roles are sacred and important. . . . Fulfilling these roles in love helps God's children progress toward eternal life" (*General Handbook* 2.1.1 as of September 2024).
18. David O. McKay, "No other success can compensate for failure in the

NOTES

home" ("Blessed are they that do His commandments," *Ensign*, May 1964).

19. Elder J Ballard Washburn taught, "We go to the temple to make covenants, but we go home to keep the covenants that we have made. The home is the testing ground" ("The Temple is a Family Affair," *Ensign*, May 1995).
20. See *General Handbook* 2.0 through 2.2.4 (as of September 2024). See also *The Family: A Proclamation to the World*.
21. See Dallin H. Oaks, "The Keys and Authority of the Priesthood," *Ensign*, May 2014.
22. Discourse, 10 March 1844, as Reported by Wilford Woodruff, 211, The Joseph Smith Papers.
23. See Dieter F. Uchtdorf, "The Infinite Power of Hope," *Ensign*, November 2008.
24. Agency is eternally central. Without agency, "there is no existence" (Doctrine and Covenants 93:30).

Appendix: Promises to Posterity

1. "Hope for Parents of Wayward Children," *Ensign*, September 2002.
2. It is unclear what the term "not transgressed" here means. It could mean the child not violating or discarding their covenant without repentance. It may also mean, in context of Joseph's sermon here and other scriptures (such as Doctrine and Covenants 132:26–27), the child "sinning" against the Holy Ghost, or the unpardonable sin.
3. "Discourse, 13 August 1843–A, as Reported by Martha Jane Knowlton Coray," [30, 33–35], The Joseph Smith Papers, https://www.josephsmithpapers.org/paper-summary/discourse-13-august-1843-a-as-reported-by-martha-jane-knowlton-coray/5; Joseph's journal records it this way: "he shall send Elijah the prophet . . . and he shall reveal the covenants of the fathrs <in relation> to the childrn,— <originally written—> and the childrn and the covena[n]ts of th[e] childr[en] in relati[o]n to the fathrs . . . doctrine of Electi[o]n sealing the father & childrn together."
4. Brigham Young, "Holy Ghost Requisite to Teach the Truth," *Journal of Discourses* 11:212.
5. in *Collected Discourses*, comp. Brian H. Stuy, 5 vols. [1987–92], 3:364.
6. Orson F. Whitney, in Conference Report, April 1929, 110.
7. *Doctrines of Salvation (Volume 2)*, compiled by Bruce R. McConkie (Bookcraft, 1955), 2:90.

NOTES

8. James E. Faust, "The Greatest Challenge in the World—Good Parenting," *Ensign*, November 1990.
9. Boyd K. Packer, "Our Moral Environment," *Ensign*, May 1992.
10. Henry B. Eyring, "Our Perfect Example," *Ensign*, November 2009.
11. David A. Bednar, "Faithful Parents and Wayward Children: Sustaining Hope While Overcoming Misunderstanding," *Ensign*, March 2014.
12. Blessing to Sarah Ann Whitney, 23 March 1843, 1, The Joseph Smith Papers, https://www.josephsmithpapers.org/paper-summary/blessing-to-sarah-ann-whitney-23-march-1843/1?highlight=own%20head#historical-intro.
13. Speaking of these divine promises, President James E. Faust said, "A principle in this [Orson F. Whitney divine tentacles] statement that is often overlooked is that they must fully repent and 'suffer for their sins' and 'pay their debt to justice'" (James E. Faust, "Dear Are the Sheep That Have Wandered," *Ensign,* May 2003, 62).
14. David A. Bednar, "Faithful Parents and Wayward Children: Sustaining Hope While Overcoming Misunderstanding," *Ensign*, March 2014.

ABOUT THE AUTHORS

ANTHONY SWEAT is a professor of Church history and doctrine at Brigham Young University. He is the author of numerous best-selling books related to the history and teachings of The Church of Jesus Christ of Latter-day Saints. He loves teaching the restored gospel to students and LDS audiences in a variety of formats. He received a BFA in painting and drawing from the University of Utah and MEd and PhD degrees in education from Utah State University.

CINDY SWEAT received her bachelor's degree in family and human development from Utah State University. After marriage and graduation, she went right to work using her education to raise seven children, spending twenty-four years straight with at least one child by her side during the day. She returned to school and in 2022 earned a master of public administration from Brigham Young University.